Root of David

NEW TESTAMENT FULFILLMENT OF OLD TESTA-MENT PROPHECIES includes many proofs that Jesus is the Messiah. These proofs include: Prophecies and fulfillments topically arranged, How Jesus fulfills the Levitical feasts, types and shadows of Christ through the Old Testament, the names for God and many, many more proofs that will help develop in you a sincere love and respect for the Word of God.

Prologue

NEW TESTAMENT
FULFILLMENT
OF
OLD TESTAMENT
PROPHECIES

Abram Kenneth Abraham

BARBOUR BOOKS
164 Mill Street
Westwood, New Jersey 07675

ISBN 1-55748-056-7

Published by: **BARBOUR AND COMPANY, INC.**
                  164 Mill Street
                  Westwood, New Jersey 07675

(In Canada, THE CHRISTIAN LIBRARY,
960 The Gateway, Burlington, Ontario L7L 5K7)

EVANGELICAL CHRISTIAN PUBLISHERS ASSOCIATION   MEMBER

Also published under the title PROMISES OF THE MESSIAH

Printed in the United States of America

TABLE OF CONTENTS

* * * *

HOW TO USE THIS BOOK

This book is a compilation of Old Testament prophecies which are fulfilled by Jesus Christ and recorded in the New Testament. Some of the Scriptures are prophecies fulfilled by specific events in the life of Jesus, while others provide valuable insights into the character and lifestyle of our Lord. In a few instances, words of explanation accompany the Scripture, but most of the prophetic fulfillments are allowed to stand alone.

The prophecies and fulfillments are arranged topically. For example if you are seeking Scripture concerning the birth of the Messiah, you will find the details regarding WHEN, WHERE, HOW, and WHY the Messiah was to be born all listed under the topic: *HIS BIRTH*. The individual prophecies and their fulfillments are grouped together. At times, several passages are used to illustrate a particular prophecy or fulfillment. In some cases, understanding is enhanced by grouping a cluster of prophecies or fulfillments with their corresponding Scriptures.

Due to its topical nature, some repetition of Scripture is necessary. Often, the same passage may yield several prophecies or fulfillments concerning the Messiah. As such, that passage may be listed under various topics to gain maximum understanding of how Jesus is shown to be the Christ.

Because of its handy format, this book may easily be used as a devotional guide, an evangelistic tool, or a topical Bible study for individuals or groups. However you choose to use it, keep in mind that the material within these pages is powerful. "For the word of God is quick, and powerful, and sharper than any two-edged sword, piercing even to the dividing asunder of soul and spirit, and of the joints and marrow, and is a discerner of the thoughts and intents of the heart" (Hebrews 4:12).

May you see Jesus within these pages. See Him as Saviour, as Prophet, Priest, and King. See Him as He is, the Anointed One, Yeshua Ha Mashiach, Jesus the Messiah!

HIS PREDECESSOR

,, The voice of him that crieth in the wilderness, Prepare ye the way of the LORD, make straight in the desert a highway for our God.

Every valley shall be exalted, and every mountain and hill shall be made low; and the crooked shall be made straight, and the rough places plain:

And the glory of the LORD shall be revealed, and all flesh shall see it together: for the mouth of the LORD hath spoken it.

Isaiah 40:3-5

Annas and Caiaphas being the high priests, the word of God came unto John the son of Zacharias in the wilderness.

And he came into all the country about Jordan, preaching the baptism of repentance for the remission of sins;

As it is written in the book of the words of Esaias the prophet, saying, The voice of one crying in the wilderness, Prepare ye the way of the Lord, make his paths straight.

Every valley shall be filled, and every mountain and hill shall be brought low; and the crooked shall be made straight, and the rough ways shall be made smooth;

And all flesh shall see the salvation of God.

Luke 3:2-6

O Zion, that bringest good tidings, get thee up into the high mountain; O Jerusalem, that bringest good tidings, lift up thy voice with strength; lift it up, be not afraid; say unto the cities of Judah, Behold your God!

Behold, the LORD God will come with strong hand, and his arm shall rule for him: behold, his reward is with him, and his work before him.

Isaiah 40:9,10

In those days came John the Baptist, preaching in the wilderness of Judaea,

And saying, Repent ye: for the kingdom of heaven is at hand.

For this is he that was spoken of by the prophet Esaias, saying, The voice of one crying in the wilderness, Prepare ye the way of the LORD, make his paths straight.

Matthew 3:1-3

* * * *

Behold, I will send my messenger, and he shall prepare the way before me: and the LORD, whom ye seek, shall suddenly come to his temple, even the messenger of the covenant, whom ye delight in: behold, he shall come, saith the LORD of hosts.

Malachi 3:1

As it is written in the prophets, Behold, I send my messenger before thy face, which shall prepare thy way before thee.

The voice of one crying in the wilderness, Prepare ye the way of the LORD, make his paths straight.

Mark 1:2, 3

And when the messengers of John were departed, he began to speak unto the people concerning John, What went ye out into the wilderness for to see? A reed shaken with the wind?

But what went ye out for to see? A man clothed in soft raiment? Behold, they which are gorgeously apparelled, and live delicately, are in king's courts.

But what went ye out for to see? A prophet? Yea, I say unto you, and much more than a prophet.

This is he, of whom it is written, Behold, I send my messenger before thy face, which shall prepare thy way before thee.

Luke 7:24-27

* * * *

Behold, I will send you Elijah the prophet before the coming of the great and dreadful day of the LORD. . .

Malachi 4:5

For this is he, of whom it is written, Behold, I send my messenger before thy face, which shall prepare thy way before thee.

For all the prophets and the law prophesied until John.

And if ye will receive it, this is Elias, which was for to come.

Matthew 11:10, 13, 14

And he shall go before him in the spirit and power of Elias,

9

to turn the hearts of the fathers to the children, and the disobedient to the wisdom of the just; to make ready a people prepared for the LORD.

Luke 1:17

He said, I am the voice of one crying in the wilderness, Make straight the way of the LORD, as said the prophet Esaias.

John 1:23

*   *   *   *

In that day will I cause the horn of the house of Israel to bud forth, and I will give thee the opening of the mouth in the midst of them; and they shall know that I am the LORD.

Ezekiel 29:21

Blessed be the LORD God of Israel; for he hath visited and redeemed his people.

And hath raised up an horn of salvation for us in the house of his servant David. . .

And thou, child, shalt be called the prophet of the Highest: for thou shalt go before the face of the LORD to prepare his ways;

To give knowledge of salvation unto his people by the remission of their sins,

Through the tender mercy of our God; whereby the dayspring from on high hath visited us,

To give light to them that sit in darkness and in the shadow of death, to guide our feet into the way of peace.

Luke 1:68-69, 76-79

HIS LINEAGE

And I will put enmity between thee and the woman, and between thy seed and her seed; it shall bruise thy head, and thou shalt bruise his heel.

Genesis 3:15

But when the fulness of the time was come, God sent forth his Son, made of a woman, made under the law . . .

Galatians 4:4

And she brought forth her firstborn son, and wrapped him in swaddling clothes, and laid him in a manger; because there was no room for them in the inn.

Luke 2:7

And she brought forth a man child, who was to rule all nations with a rod of iron: and her child was caught up unto God, and to his throne.

Revelation 12:5

* * * *

And I will bless them that bless thee, and curse him that curseth thee: and in thee shall all families of the earth be blessed.

Genesis 12:3

The book of the generation of Jesus Christ, the son of David, the son of Abraham.

Matthew 1:1

Which was the son of Jacob, which was the son of Isaac, which was the son of Abraham, which was the son of Thara, which was the son of Nachor . . .

Luke 3:34

* * * *

For all the land which thou seest, to thee will I give it, and to thy seed for ever.

Genesis 13:15

And Abram fell on his face: and God talked with him, saying . . .

11

And I will establish my covenant between me and thee and thy seed after thee in their generations for an everlasting covenant, to be a God unto thee, and to thy seed after thee.

Genesis 17:3, 7

Now to Abraham and his seed were the promises made. He saith not, And to seeds, as of many; but as of one, And to thy seed, which is Christ.

Galatians 3:16

Whose are the fathers, and of whom as concerning the flesh Christ came, who is over all, God blessed for ever. Amen.

Romans 9:5

Seeing that Abraham shall surely become a great and mighty nation, and all the nations of the earth shall be blessed in him?

Genesis 18:18

And in thy seed shall all the nations of the earth be blessed; because thou hast obeyed my voice.

Genesis 22:18

Ye are the children of the prophets, and of the covenant which God made with our fathers, saying unto Abraham, And in thy seed shall all the kindreds of the earth be blessed.

Acts 3:25

For ye are all the children of God by faith in Christ Jesus. . .

And if ye be Christ's, then are ye Abraham's seed, and heirs according to the promise.

Galatians 3:26, 29

Blessed be the LORD God of Israel; for he hath visited and redeemed his people . . .

As he spake by the mouth of his holy prophets, which have been since the world began:

That we should be saved from our enemies, and from the hand of all that hate us;

To perform the mercy promised to our fathers, and to remember his holy convenant;

The oath which he sware to our father Abraham,

That he would grant unto us, that we being delivered out of the hand of our enemies might serve him without fear,

In holiness and righteousness before him, all the days of our life.

Luke 1:68, 70-75

* * * *

And God said, Sarah thy wife shall bear thee a son indeed; and thou shalt call his name Isaac: and I will establish my covenant with him for an everlasting covenant, and with his seed after him.

Genesis 17:19

And God said unto Abraham, Let it not be grievous in thy sight because of the lad, and because of thy bondwoman; in all that Sarah hath said unto thee, hearken unto her voice, for in Isaac shall thy seed be called.

Genesis 21:12

Abraham begat Isaac; and Isaac begat Jacob; and Jacob begat Judas and his brethren...

Matthew 1:2

And Jesus himself began to be about thirty years of age, being (as was supposed) the son of Joseph, which was the son of Heli...

Which was the son of Jacob, which was the son of Isaac, which was the son of Abraham, which was the son of Thara, which was the son of Nachor . . .

Luke 3:23, 34

Not as though the word of God hath taken none effect. For they are not all Israel, which are of Israel:

Neither, because they are the seed of Abraham, are they all children: but, In Isaac shall thy seed be called.

That is, They which are the children of the flesh, these are not the children of God: but the children of the promise are counted for the seed.

For this is the word of promise, At this time will I come, and Sarah shall have a son.

Romans 9:6-9

* * * *

And, behold, the LORD stood above it, and said, I am the LORD God of Abraham thy father, and the God of Isaac: the land whereon thou liest, to thee will I give it, and to thy seed;

And thy seed shall be as the dust of the earth, and thou shalt spread abroad to the west, and to the east, and to the north, and to the south: and in thee and in thy seed shall all the families of the earth be blessed.

Genesis 28:13, 14

And God said unto him, Thy name is Jacob: thy name shall not be called any more Jacob, but Israel shall be thy name: and he called his name Israel.

And God said unto him, I am God Almighty: be fruitful and multiply; a nation and a company of nations shall be of thee, and kings shall come out of thy loins;

And the land which I gave Abraham and Isaac, to thee I will give it, and to thy seed after thee will I give the land.

Genesis 35:10-12

I shall see him, but not now: I shall behold him, but not nigh: there shall come a Star out of Jacob, and a Sceptre shall rise out of Israel, and shall smite the corners of Moab, and destroy all the children of Sheth.

Numbers 24:17

Abraham begat Isaac; and Isaac begat Jacob; and Jacob begat Judas and his brethren . . .

Matthew 1:2

Which was the son of Jacob, which was the son of Isaac, which was the son of Abraham, which was the son of Thara, which was the son of Nachor . . .

Luke 3:34

*   *   *   *

Judah, thou art he whom thy brethren shall praise: thy hand shall be in the neck of thine enemies; thy father's children shall bow down before thee.

Judah is a lion's whelp: from the prey, my son, thou art gone up: he stooped down, he couched as a lion, and as an old lion; who shall rouse him up?

The sceptre shall not depart from Judah, nor a lawgiver from between his feet, until Shiloh come; and unto him shall the gathering of the people be.

Genesis 49:8-10

But thou, Bethlehem Ephratah, though thou be little among the thousands of Judah, yet out of thee shall he come forth unto me that is to be ruler in Israel; whose goings forth have been from of old, from everlasting.

Micah 5:2

And Jesus himself began to be about thirty years of age, being (as was supposed) the son of Joseph, which was the son of Heli . . . Which was the son of Aminadab which was the son of Aram, which was the son of Esrom, which was the son of Phares, which was the son of Juda.

Luke 3:23, 33

For it is evident that our LORD sprang out of Juda; of which tribe Moses spake nothing concerning priesthood.

Hebrews 7:14

And one of the elders saith unto me, Weep not: behold, the Lion of the tribe of Juda, the Root of David, hath prevailed to open the book, and to loose the seven seals thereof.

Revelation 5:5

* * *

And there shall come forth a rod out of the stem of Jesse, and a Branch shall grow out of his roots . . .

Isaiah 11:1

And Jesus himself began to be about thirty years of age, being (as was supposed) the son of Joseph, which was the son of Heli . . .

Which was the son of Jesse, which was the son of Obed, which was the son of Booz, which was the son of Salmon, which was the son of Naasson,

Luke 3:23, 32

* * * *

15

And when thy days be fulfilled, and thou shalt sleep with thy fathers, I will set up thy seed after thee, which shall proceed out of thy bowels, and I will establish his kingdom.

He shall build an house for my name, and I will stablish the throne of his kingdom for ever.

I will be his father, and he shall be my son. If he commit iniquity, I will chasten him with the rod of men, and with the stripes of the children of men:

But my mercy shall not depart away from him, as I took it from Saul, whom I put away before thee.

And thine house and thy kingdom shall be established for ever before thee: thy throne shall be established for ever.

According to all these words, and according to all this vision, so did Nathan speak unto David.

2 Samuel 7:12-17

Behold, the days come, saith the LORD, that I will raise unto David a righteous Branch, and a King shall reign and prosper, and shall execute judgment and justice in the earth . . .

In those days, and at that time, will I cause the Branch of righteousness to grow up unto David; and he shall execute judgment and righteousness in the land.

Jeremiah 23:5, 33:15

And, behold, thou shalt conceive in thy womb, and bring forth a son, and shalt call his name Jesus.

He shall be great, and shall be called the Son of the Highest: and the LORD God shall give unto him the throne of his father David:

And he shall reign over the house of Jacob for ever; and of his kingdom there shall be no end.

Luke 1:31-33

And Jesus himself began to be about thirty years of age, being (as was supposed) the son of Joseph, which was the son of Heli. . .

Which was the son of Simeon, which was the son of Juda, which was the son of Joseph, which was the son of Jonan, which was the son of Eliakim,

Which was the son of Melea, which was the son of Menan, which was the son of Mattatha, which was the son of Nathan,

16

which was the son of David . . .

Luke 3:23, 30, 31

The book of the generation of Jesus Christ, the son of David, the son of Abraham.

Matthew 1:1

And when Jesus departed thence, two blind men followed him, crying, and saying, Thou Son of David, have mercy on us.

Matthew 9:27

And, behold, a woman of Canaan came out of the same coasts, and cried unto him, saying, Have mercy on me, O LORD, thou son of David; my daughter is grievously vexed with a devil.

Matthew 15:22

And when he heard that it was Jesus of Nazareth, he began to cry out, and say, Jesus, thou son of David, have mercy on me.

Mark 10:47

And when he had removed him, he raised up unto them David to be their king; to whom also he gave testimony, and said, I have found David the son of Jesse, a man after mine own heart, which shall fulfil all my will.

Of this man's seed hath God according to his promise raised unto Israel a Saviour, Jesus:

Acts 13:22, 23

Concerning his Son Jesus Christ our LORD, which was made of the seed of David according to the flesh;

Romans 1:3

I Jesus have sent mine angel to testify unto you these things in the churches. I am the root and the offspring of David, and the bright and morning star.

Revelation 22:16

17

HIS BIRTH
(and accompanying events)

Now gather thyself in troops, O daughter of troops: he hath laid siege against us: they shall smite the judge of Israel with a rod upon the cheek.

But thou, Bethlehem Ephratah, though thou be little among the thousands of Judah, yet out of thee shall he come forth unto me that is to be ruler in Israel; whose goings forth have been from of old, from everlasting.

Therefore will he give them up, until the time that she which travaileth hath brought forth: then the remnant of his brethren shall return unto the children of Israel.

Micah 5:1-3

Now when Jesus was born in Bethlehem of Judaea in the days of Herod the king, behold, there came wise men from the east to Jerusalem,

Saying, Where is he that is born King of the Jews? for we have seen his star in the east, and are come to worship him.

When Herod the king had heard these things, he was troubled, and all Jerusalem with him.

And when he had gathered all the chief priests and scribes of the people together, he demanded of them where Christ should be born.

And they said unto him, In Bethlehem of Judaea: for thus it is written by the prophet,

And thou Bethlehem, in the land of Juda, art not the least among the princes of Juda: for out of thee shall come a Governor, that shall rule my people Israel.

Matthew 2:1-6

And Joseph also went up from Galilee, out of the city of Nazareth, into Judaea, unto the city of David, which is called Bethlehem; (because he was of the house and lineage of David:)

To be taxed with Mary his espoused wife, being great with child. . .

And she brought forth her firstborn son, and wrapped him in swaddling clothes, and laid him in a manger; because there was no room for them in the inn. . .

18

And it came to pass, as the angels were gone away from them into heaven, the shepherds said one to another, Let us now go even unto Bethlehem, and see this thing which is come to pass, which the LORD hath made known unto us.

Luke 2:4, 5, 7, 15

Hath not the scripture said, That Christ cometh of the seed of David, and out of the town of Bethlehem, where David was?

John 7:42

Seventy weeks are determined upon thy people and upon thy holy city, to finish the transgression, and to make an end of sins, and to make reconciliation for iniquity, and to bring in everlasting righteousness, and to seal up the vision and prophecy, and to anoint the most Holy.

Know therefore and understand, that from the going forth of the commandment to restore and to build Jerusalem unto the Messiah the Prince shall be seven weeks, and threescore and two weeks: the street shall be built again, and the wall, even in troublous times.

Daniel 9:24, 25

The sceptre shall not depart from Judah, nor a lawgiver from between his feet, until Shiloh come; and unto him shall the gathering of the people be.

Genesis 49:10

I shall see him, but not now: I shall behold him, but not nigh: there shall come a Star out of Jacob, and a Sceptre shall rise out of Israel, and shall smite the corners of Moab, and destroy all the children of Sheth.

Numbers 24:17

Behold, I will send my messenger, and he shall prepare the way before me: and the LORD, whom ye seek, shall suddenly come to his temple, even the messenger of the covenant, whom ye delight in: behold, he shall come, saith the LORD of hosts.

Malachi 3:1

And it came to pass in those days, that there went out a decree from Caesar Augustus, that all the world should be taxed.

(And this taxing was first made when Cyrenius was governor of Syria.)

And all went to be taxed, every one into his own city.

And Joseph also went up from Galilee, out of the city of Nazareth, into Judaea, unto the city of David, which is called Bethlehem; (because he was of the house and lineage of David:)

To be taxed with Mary his espoused wife, being great with child.

Luke 2:1-5

* * * *

Therefore the LORD himself shall give you a sign; Behold, a virgin shall conceive, and bear a son, and shall call his name Immanuel. . .

For unto us a child is born, unto us a son is given: and the government shall be upon his shoulder: and his name shall be called Wonderful, Counsellor, The mighty God, The everlasting Father, The Prince of Peace.

Of the increase of his government and peace there shall be no end, upon the throne of David, and upon his kingdom, to order it, and to establish it with judgment and with justice from henceforth even for ever. The zeal of the LORD of hosts will perform this.

Isaiah 7:14, 9:6-7

And in the sixth month the angel Gabriel was sent from God unto a city of Galilee, named Nazareth,

To a virgin espoused to a man whose name was Joseph, of the house of David; and the virgin's name was Mary. . .

And the angel said unto her, Fear not, Mary: for thou hast found favour with God.

And, behold, thou shalt conceive in thy womb, and bring forth a son, and shalt call his name JESUS.

He shall be great, and shall be called the Son of the Highest: and the LORD God shall give unto him the throne of his father David:

And he shall reign over the house of Jacob for ever; and of his kingdom there shall be no end.

Then said Mary unto the angel, How shall this be, seeing I know not a man?

20

And the angel answered and said unto her, The Holy Ghost shall come upon thee, and the power of the Highest shall overshadow thee: therefore also that holy thing which shall be born of thee shall be called the Son of God.

Luke 1:26, 27, 30-35

And she brought forth her firstborn son, and wrapped him in swaddling clothes, and laid him in a manger; because there was no room for them in the inn. . .

And the angel said unto them, Fear not: for, behold, I bring you good tidings of great joy, which shall be to all people.

For unto you is born this day in the city of David a Saviour, which is Christ the LORD.

Luke 2:7, 10, 11

And she shall bring forth a son, and thou shalt call his name JESUS: for he shall save his people from their sins.

Now all this was done, that it might be fulfilled which was spoken of the LORD by the prophet, saying,

Behold, a virgin shall be with child, and shall bring forth a son, and they shall call his name Emmanuel, which being interpreted is, God with us.

Matthew 1:21-23

And there came a fear on all: and they glorified God, saying, That a great prophet is risen up among us; and, That God hath visited his people.

Luke 7:16

* * * *

The kings of Tarshish and of the isles shall bring presents: the kings of Sheba and Seba shall offer gifts.

Yea, all kings shall fall down before him: all nations shall serve him.

For he shall deliver the needy when he crieth; the poor also, and him that hath no helper.

He shall spare the poor and needy, and shall save the souls of the needy.

He shall redeem their soul from deceit and violence: and precious shall their blood be in his sight.

21

And he shall live, and to him shall be given of the gold of Sheba: prayer also shall be made for him continually; and daily shall he be praised.

Psalms 72:10-15

In that time shall the present be brought unto the LORD of hosts of a people scattered and peeled, and from a people terrible from their beginning hitherto; a nation meted out and trodden under foot, whose land the rivers have spoiled, to the place of the name of the LORD of hosts, the mount Zion.

Isaiah 18:7

And the Gentiles shall come to thy light, and kings to the brightness of thy rising. . .

All the flocks of Kedar shall be gathered together unto thee, the rams of Nebaioth shall minister unto thee: they shall come up with acceptance on mine altar, and I will glorify the house of my glory.

Isaiah 60:3, 7

Now when Jesus was born in Bethlehem of Judaea in the days of Herod the king, behold, there came wise men from the east to Jerusalem,

Saying, Where is he that is born King of the Jews? for we have seen his star in the east, and are come to worship him.

Matthew 2:1, 2

Then Herod, when he had privily called the wise men, enquired of them diligently what time the star appeared.

And he sent them to Bethlehem, and said, Go and search diligently for the young child; and when ye have found him, bring me word again, that I may come and worship him also.

When they had heard the king, they departed; and, lo, the star, which they saw in the east, went before them, till it came and stood over where the young child was.

When they saw the star, they rejoiced with exceeding great joy.

And when they were come into the house, they saw the young child with Mary his mother, and fell down, and worshipped him: and when they had opened their treasures, they presented unto him gifts: gold, and frankincense, and myrrh.

Matthew 2:7-11

I will declare the decree: the LORD hath said unto me, Thou art my Son; this day have I begotten thee.

Psalm 2:7

And the angel answered and said unto her, The Holy Ghost shall come upon thee, and the power of the Highest shall overshadow thee: therefore also that holy thing which shall be born of thee shall be called the Son of God.

Luke 1:35

* * * *

Because thou hast made the LORD, which is my refuge, even the most High, thy habitation;
There shall no evil befall thee, neither shall any plague come nigh thy dwelling.
For he shall give his angels charge over thee, to keep thee in all thy ways.

Psalm 91:9-11

And being warned of God in a dream that they should not return to Herod, they departed into their own country another way.

Matthew 2:12

* * * *

When Israel was a child, then I loved him, and called my son out of Egypt.

Hosea 11:1

And when they were departed, behold, the angel of the LORD appeareth to Joseph in a dream, saying, Arise, and take the young child and his mother, and flee into Egypt; and be thou there until I bring thee word: for Herod will seek the young child to destroy him.
When he arose, he took the young child and his mother by night, and departed into Egypt:

23

And was there until the death of Herod: that it might be fulfilled which was spoken of the LORD by the prophet, saying, Out of Egypt have I called my son.

Matthew 2:13-15

* * * *

Thus saith the LORD; A voice was heard in Ramah, lamentation, and bitter weeping; Rahel weeping for her children refused to be comforted for her children, because they were not.

Jeremiah 31:15

Then Herod, when he saw that he was mocked of the wise men, was exceeding wroth, and sent forth, and slew all the children that were in Bethlehem, and in all the coasts thereof, from two years old and under, according to the time which he had diligently enquired of the wise men.

Then was fulfilled that which was spoken by Jeremy the prophet, saying,

In Rama was there a voice heard, lamentation, and weeping, and great mourning, Rachel weeping for her children, and would not be comforted, because they are not.

Matthew 2:16-18

* * * *

Nevertheless the dimness shall not be such as was in her vexation, when at the first he lightly afflicted the land of Zebulun and the land of Naphtali, and afterward did more grievously afflict her by the way of the sea, beyond Jordan, in Galilee of the nations.

The people that walked in darkness have seen a great light: they that dwell in the land of the shadow of death, upon them hath the light shined.

Isaiah 9:1-2

But when Herod was dead, behold, an angel of the LORD appeareth in a dream to Joseph in Egypt,

Saying, Arise, and take the young child and his mother,

and go into the land of Israel: for they are dead which sought the young child's life.

And he arose, and took the young child and his mother, and came into the land of Israel.

But when he heard that Archelaus did reign in Judaea in the room of his father Herod, he was afraid to go thither: notwithstanding, being warned of God in a dream, he turned aside into the parts of Galilee:

And he came and dwelt in a city called Nazareth: that it might be fulfilled which was spoken by the prophets, He shall be called a Nazarene.

Matthew 2:19-23

And leaving Nazareth, he came and dwelt in Capernaum, which is upon the sea coast, in the borders of Zabulon and Nephthalim:

That it might be fulfilled which was spoken by Esaias the prophet, saying,

The land of Zabulon, and the land of Nephthalim, by the way of the sea, beyond Jordan, Galilee of the Gentiles;

The people which sat in darkness saw great light; and to them which sat in the region and shadow of death light is sprung up.

Matthew 4:13-16

HIS ANOINTING

Thy throne, O God, is for ever and ever: the sceptre of thy kingdom is a right sceptre.

Psalm 45:6

Of old hast thou laid the foundation of the earth: and the heavens are the work of thy hands.

They shall perish, but thou shalt endure: yea, all of them shall wax old like a garment; as a vesture shalt thou change them, and they shall be changed:

But thou art the same, and thy years shall have no end.

Psalm 102:25-27

But unto the Son he saith, Thy throne, O God, is for ever and ever: a sceptre of righteousness is the sceptre of thy kingdom.

Thou hast loved righteousness, and hated iniquity; therefore God, even thy God, hath anointed thee with the oil of gladness above thy fellows.

And, Thou, LORD, in the beginning hast laid the foundation of the earth; and the heavens are the works of thine hands:

They shall perish; but thou remainest; and they all shall wax old as doth a garment;

And as a vesture shalt thou fold them up, and they shall be changed: but thou art the same, and thy years shall not fail.

Hebrews 1:8-12

*   *   *   *

The Spirit of the LORD God is upon me; because the LORD hath anointed me to preach good tidings unto the meek; he hath sent me to bind up the brokenhearted, to proclaim liberty to the captives, and the opening of the prison to them that are bound;

To proclaim the acceptable year of the LORD, and the day of vengeance of our God; to comfort all that mourn;

To appoint unto them that mourn in Zion, to give unto them beauty for ashes, the oil of joy for mourning, the garment of praise for the spirit of heaviness; that they might be called trees of righteousness, the planting of the LORD, that he might be glorified.

Isaiah 61:1-3

And he came to Nazareth, where he had been brought up: and, as his custom was, he went into the synagogue on the sabbath day, and stood up for to read.

And there was delivered unto him the book of the prophet Esaias. And when he had opened the book, he found the place where it was written,

The Spirit of the LORD is upon me, because he hath anointed me to preach the gospel to the poor; he hath sent me to heal the brokenhearted, to preach deliverance to the captives, and recovering of sight to the blind, to set at liberty them that are bruised,

To preach the acceptable year of the LORD.

And he closed the book, and he gave it again to the minister, and sat down. And the eyes of all them that were in the synagogue were fastened on him.

And he began to say unto them, This day is this scripture fulfilled in your ears.

Luke 4:16-21

And there shall come forth a rod out of the stem of Jesse, and a Branch shall grow out of his roots:

And the spirit of the LORD shall rest upon him, the spirit of wisdom and understanding, the spirit of counsel and might, the spirit of knowledge and of the fear of the LORD;

And shall make him of quick understanding in the fear of the LORD: and he shall not judge after the sight of his eyes, neither reprove after the hearing of his ears:

But with righteousness shall he judge the poor, and reprove with equity for the meek of the earth: and he shall smite the earth with the rod of his mouth, and with the breath of his lips shall he slay the wicked.

Isaiah 11:1-4

Now when all the people were baptized, it came to pass, that Jesus also being baptized, and praying, the heaven was opened,

And the Holy Ghost descended in a bodily shape like a

dove upon him, and a voice came from heaven, which said, Thou art my beloved Son; in thee I am well pleased.

Luke 3:21,22

For he whom God hath sent speaketh the words of God: for God giveth not the Spirit by measure unto him.

John 3:34

* * * *

Behold my servant, whom I uphold; mine elect, in whom my soul delighteth; I have put my spirit upon him: he shall bring forth judgment to the Gentiles.

Isaiah 42:1

And Jesus, when he was baptized, went up straightway out of the water: and, lo, the heavens were opened unto him, and he saw the Spirit of God descending like a dove, and lighting upon him:

And lo a voice from heaven, saying, This is my beloved Son, in whom I am well pleased.

Matthew 3:16,17

Behold my servant, whom I have chosen; my beloved, in whom my soul is well pleased: I will put my spirit upon him, and he shall shew judgment to the Gentiles.

Matthew 12:18

And John bare record, saying, I saw the Spirit descending from heaven like a dove, and it abode upon him.

And I knew him not: but he that sent me to baptize with water, the same said unto me, Upon whom thou shalt see the Spirit descending, and remaining on him, the same is he which baptizeth with the Holy Ghost.

And I saw, and bare record that this is the Son of God.

John 1:32-34

HIS TEMPTATION

And he humbled thee, and suffered thee to hunger, and fed thee with manna, which thou knewest not, neither did thy fathers know; that he might make thee know that man doth not live by bread only, but by every word that proceedeth out of the mouth of the LORD doth man live.

Deuteronomy 8:3

And when the tempter came to him, he said, If thou be the Son of God, command that these stones be made bread.

But he answered and said, It is written, Man shall not live by bread alone, but by every word that proceedeth out of the mouth of God.

Matthew 4:3, 4

* * * *

For he shall give his angels charge over thee, to keep thee in all thy ways.

They shall bear thee up in their hands, lest thou dash thy foot against a stone.

Psalm 91:11-12

Then the devil taketh him up into the holy city, and setteth him on a pinnacle of the temple,

And saith unto him, If thou be the Son of God, cast thyself down: for it is written, He shall give his angels charge concerning thee: and in their hands they shall bear thee up, lest at any time thou dash thy foot against a stone.

Jesus said unto him, It is written again, Thou shalt not tempt the LORD thy God.

Matthew 4:5-7

* * * *

Thou shalt fear the LORD thy God, and serve him, and shalt swear by his name.

Deuteronomy 6:13

Again, the devil taketh him up into an exceeding high mountain, and sheweth him all the kingdoms of the world, and the glory of them;

And saith unto him, All these things will I give thee, if thou wilt fall down and worship me.

Then saith Jesus unto him, Get thee hence, Satan: for it is written, Thou shalt worship the LORD thy God, and him only shalt thou serve.

Then the devil leaveth him, and, behold, angels came and ministered unto him.

Matthew 4:8-11

For in that he himself hath suffered being tempted, he is able to succour them that are tempted.

Hebrews 2:18

For we have not an high priest which cannot be touched with the feeling of our infirmities; but was in all points tempted like as we are, yet without sin.

Hebrews 4:15

HIS MINISTRY

And their nobles shall be of themselves, and their governor shall proceed from the midst of them; and I will cause him to draw near, and he shall approach unto me: for who is this that engaged his heart to approach unto me? saith the LORD.

Jeremiah 30:21

And he went out from thence, and came into his own country; and his disciples follow him.

And when the sabbath day was come, he began to teach in the synagogue: and many hearing him were astonished, saying, From whence hath this man these things? and what wisdom is this which is given unto him, that even such mighty works are wrought by his hands?

Is not this the carpenter, the son of Mary, the brother of James, and Joses, and of Juda, and Simon? and are not his sisters here with us? And they were offended at him.

But Jesus said unto them, A prophet is not without honour, but in his own country, and among his own kin, and in his own house.

Mark 6:1-4

The spirit of the LORD God is upon me; because the LORD hath anointed me to preach good tidings unto the meek; he hath sent me to bind up the brokenhearted, to proclaim liberty to the captives, and the opening of the prison to them that are bound;

To proclaim the acceptable year of the LORD, and the day of vengeance of our God; to comfort all that mourn;

To appoint unto them that mourn in Zion, to give unto them beauty for ashes, the oil of joy for mourning, the garment of praise for the spirit of heaviness; that they might be called trees of righteousness, the planting of the LORD, that he might be glorified.

Isaiah 61:1-4

From that time Jesus began to preach, and to say, Repent: for the kingdom of heaven is at hand.

Matthew 4:17

Now after that John was put in prison, Jesus came into Galilee, preaching the gospel of the kingdom of God,

And saying, The time is fulfilled, and the kingdom of God is at hand: repent ye, and believe the gospel.

Mark 1:14, 15

And there was delivered unto him the book of the prophet Esaias. And when he had opened the book, he found the place where it was written,

The Spirit of the LORD is upon me, because he hath anointed me to preach the gospel to the poor; he hath sent me to heal the brokenhearted, to preach deliverance to the captives, and recovering of sight to the blind, to set at liberty them that are bruised.

To preach the acceptable year of the LORD.

And he closed the book, and he gave it again to the minister, and sat down. And the eyes of all them that were in the synagogue were fastened on him.

And he began to say unto them, This day is this scripture fulfilled in your ears.

Luke 4:17-21

*   *   *   *

Nevertheless the dimness shall not be such as was in her vexation, when at the first he lightly afflicted the land of Zebulun and the land of Naphtali, and afterward did more grievously afflict her by the way of sea, beyond Jordan, in Galilee of the nations.

The people that walked in darkness have seen a great light: they that dwell in the land of the shadow of death, upon them hath the light shined.

Isaiah 9:1, 2

Now when Jesus had heard that John was cast into prison, he departed into Galilee;

And leaving Nazareth, he came and dwelt in Capernaum, which is upon the sea coast, in the borders of Zabulon and Nephthalim:

That it might be fulfilled which was spoken by Esaias the prophet, saying,

The land of Zabulon, and the land of Nephthalim, by the way of the sea, beyond Jordan, Galilee of the Gentiles;

The people which sat in darkness saw great light; and to them which sat in the region and shadow of death light is sprung up.

From that time Jesus began to preach, and to say, Repent: for the kingdom of heaven is at hand.

Matthew 4:12-17

* * * *

I will open my mouth in a parable: I will utter dark sayings of old:

Which we have heard and known, and our fathers have told us.

We will not hide them from their children, shewing to the generation to come the praises of the LORD, and his strength, and his wonderful works that he hath done.

Psalm 78:2-4

All these things spake Jesus unto the multitude in parables; and without a parable spake he not unto them:

That it might be fulfilled which was spoken by the prophet, saying, I will open my mouth in parables; I will utter things which have been kept secret from the foundation of the world.

Matthew 13:34, 35

* * * *

Out of the mouths of babes and sucklings hast thou ordained strength because of thine enemies, that thou mightest still the enemy and the avenger.

Psalm 8:2

And when the chief priests and scribes saw the wonderful things that he did, and the children crying in the temple, and saying, Hosanna to the son of David; they were sore displeased. . .

Matthew 21:15

* * * *

Behold, I will send my messenger, and he shall prepare the way before me: and the LORD, whom ye seek, shall suddenly come to his temple, even the messenger of the covenant, whom ye delight in: behold, he shall come, saith the LORD of hosts.

Malachi 3:1

And Jesus went into the temple of God, and cast out all them that sold and bought in the temple, and overthrew the tables of the moneychangers, and the seats of them that sold doves. . .

Matthew 21:12

* * * *

For the zeal of thine house hath eaten me up; and the reproaches of them that reproached thee are fallen upon me.

Psalm 69:9

My zeal hath consumed me, because mine enemies have forgotten thy words.

Psalm 119:139

And the Jews' passover was at hand, and Jesus went up to Jerusalem,

And found in the temple those that sold oxen and sheep and doves, and the changers of money sitting:

And when he had made a scourge of small cords, he drove them all out of the temple, and the sheep, and the oxen; and poured out the changers' money, and overthrew the tables;

And said unto them that sold doves, Take these things hence; make not my Father's house a house of merchandise.

And his disciples remembered that it was written, The zeal of thine house hath eaten me up.

John 2:13-17

Behold my servant, whom I uphold; mine elect, in whom my soul delighteth; I have put my spirit upon him: he shall bring forth judgment to the Gentiles. . .

I the LORD have called thee in righteousness, and will hold thine hand, and will keep thee, and give thee for a covenant of the people, for a light of the Gentiles.

Isaiah 42:1, 6

A light to lighten the Gentiles, and the glory of thy people Israel.

Luke 2:32

For so hath the LORD commanded us, saying, I have set thee to be a light of the Gentiles, that thou shouldest be for salvation unto the ends of the earth.

Acts 13:47

*　*　*　*

And in that day there shall be a root of Jesse, which shall stand for an ensign of the people; to it shall the Gentiles seek: and his rest shall be glorious.

Isaiah 11:10

And that the Gentiles might glorify God for his mercy; as it is written, For this cause I will confess to thee among the Gentiles, and sing unto thy name.

And again he saith, Rejoice, ye Gentiles, with his people.

And again, Praise the LORD, all ye Gentiles; and laud him, all ye people.

And again, Esaias saith, There shall be a root of Jesse, and he that shall rise to reign over the Gentiles; in him shall the Gentiles trust.

Romans 15:9-12

*　*　*　*

I delight to do thy will, O my God: yea, thy law is within my heart.

Psalm 40:8

Jesus saith unto them, My meat is to do the will of him that sent me, and to finish his work.

John 4:34

HIS DEATH PREDICTED

Awake, O sword, against my shepherd, and against the man that is my fellow, saith the LORD of hosts: smite the shepherd, and the sheep shall be scattered: and I will turn mine hand upon the little ones.

Zechariah 13:7

I am the good shepherd: the good shepherd giveth his life for the sheep.

As the Father knoweth me, even so know I the Father: and I lay down my life for the sheep.

John 10:11, 15

*   *   *   *

Mine enemies reproach me all the day; and they that are mad against me are sworn against me.

For I have eaten ashes like bread, and mingled my drink with weeping,

Because of thine indignation and thy wrath: for thou hast lifted me up, and cast me down.

Psalm 102:8-10

Then said Jesus unto them, When ye have lifted up the Son of man, then shall ye know that I am he, and that I do nothing of myself; but as my Father hath taught me, I speak these things.

John 8:28

And as Moses lifted up the serpent in the wilderness, even so must the Son of man be lifted up.

John 3:14

And I, if I be lifted up from the earth, will draw all men unto me.

John 12:32

*   *   *   *

Therefore will I divide him a portion with the great, and

36

he shall divide the spoil with the strong; because he hath poured out his soul unto death: and he was numbered with the transgressors; and he bare the sin of many, and made intercession for the transgressors.

Isaiah 53:12

For I say unto you, that this that is written must yet be accomplished in me, And he was reckoned among the transgressors: for the things concerning me have an end.

Luke 22:37

And with him they crucify two thieves; the one on his right hand, and the other on his left.

And the scripture was fulfilled, which saith, And he was numbered with the transgressors.

Mark 15:27, 28

* * * *

My God, my God, why hast thou forsaken me? why art thou so far from helping me, and from the words of my roaring?

Psalm 22:1

And about the ninth hour Jesus cried with a loud voice, saying, Eli, Eli, la-ma sa-bach-tha-ni? that is to say, My God, my God, why hast thou forsaken me?

Matthew 27:46

* * * *

All they that see me laugh me to scorn: they shoot out the lip, they shake the head, saying,

He trusted on the LORD that he would deliver him: let him deliver him, seeing he delighted in him.

Psalm 22:7

I became also a reproach unto them: when they looked upon me they shaked their heads.

Psalm 109:25

And they that passed by reviled him, wagging their heads,
And saying, Thou that destroyest the temple, and buildest

37

it in three days, save thyself. If thou be the Son of God, come down from the cross.

Matthew 27:39, 40

And they that passed by railed on him, wagging their heads, and saying, Ah, thou that destroyest the temple, and buildest it in three days,

Save thyself, and come down from the cross.

Likewise also the chief priests mocking said among themselves with the scribes, He saved others; himself he cannot save.

Let Christ the King of Israel descend now from the cross, that we may see and believe. And they that were crucified with him reviled him.

Mark 15:29-32

* * * *

They part my garments among them, and cast lots upon my vesture.

Psalm 22:18

Then said Jesus, Father, forgive them; for they know not what they do. And they parted his raiment, and cast lots.

Luke 23:34

He keepeth all his bones: not one of them is broken.

Psalm 34:20

In one house shall it be eaten; thou shalt not carry forth aught of the flesh abroad out of the house; neither shall ye break a bone thereof.

Exodus 12:46

Then came the soldiers, and brake the legs of the first, and of the other which was crucified with him.

But when they came to Jesus, and saw that he was dead already, they brake not his legs. . .

For these things were done, that the scripture should be fulfilled, A bone of him shall not be broken.

John 19:32, 33, 36

* * * *

They gave me also gall for my meat; and in my thirst they gave me vinegar to drink.

Psalm 69:21

They gave him vinegar to drink mingled with gall: and when he had tasted thereof, he would not drink.

Matthew 27:34

But he was wounded for our transgressions, he was bruised for our iniquities: the chastisement of our peace was upon him; and with his stripes we are healed.

Isaiah 53:5

For he hath made him to be sin for us, who knew no sin; that we might be made the righteousness of God in him.

2 Corinthians 5:21

HIS TRIUMPHANT ENTRY INTO JERUSALEM

Rejoice greatly, O daughter of Zion; shout, O daughter of Jerusalem: behold, thy King cometh unto thee: he is just, and having salvation; lowly, and riding upon an ass, and upon a colt the foal of an ass.

Zechariah 9:9

And they brought him to Jesus: and they cast their garments upon the colt, and they set Jesus thereon.

And as he went, they spread their clothes in the way.

And when he was come nigh, even now at the descent of the mount of Olives, the whole multitude of the disciples began to rejoice and praise God with a loud voice for all the mighty works that they had seen.

Luke 19:35-37

And a very great multitude spread their garments in the way; others cut down branches from the trees, and strawed them in the way.

And the multitudes that went before, and that followed, cried, saying, Hosanna to the son of David: Blessed is he that cometh in the name of the LORD; Hosanna in the highest.

And when he was come into Jerusalem, all the city was moved, saying, Who is this?

And the multitude said, This is Jesus the prophet of Nazareth of Galilee.

Matthew 21:8-11

* * * *

Out of the mouth of babes and sucklings hast thou ordained strength because of thine enemies, that thou mightest still the enemy and the avenger.

Psalm 8:2

And when the chief priests and scribes saw the wonderful things that he did, and the children crying in the temple, and saying, Hosanna to the son of David; they were sore displeased,

And said unto him, Hearest thou what these say? And Jesus saith unto them, Yea; have ye never read, Out of the mouth of babes and sucklings thou hast perfected praise?

Matthew 21:15, 16

* * * *

Save now, I beseech thee, O LORD: O LORD, I beseech thee, send now prosperity.

Blessed be he that cometh in the name of the LORD: we have blessed you out of the house of the LORD.

Psalm 118:25, 26

And they brought the colt to Jesus, and cast their garments on him; and he sat upon him.

And many spread their garments in the way: and others cut down branches off the trees, and strawed them in the way.

And they that went before, and they that followed, cried, saying, Hosanna; Blessed is he that cometh in the name of the LORD:

Blessed be the kingdom of our father David, that cometh in the name of the LORD: Hosanna in the highest.

Mark 11:7-10

41

HIS REJECTION

Who hath believed our report? and to whom is the arm of the LORD revealed?

Isaiah 53:1

But though he had done so many miracles before them, yet they believed not on him:

That the saying of Esaias the prophet might be fulfilled, which he spake, LORD, who hath believed our report? and to whom hath the arm of the LORD been revealed?

Therefore they could not believe, because that Esaias said again,

He hath blinded their eyes, and hardened their heart; that they should not see with their eyes, nor understand with their heart, and be converted, and I should heal them.

These things said Esaias, when he saw his glory, and spake of him.

John 12:37-41

* * * *

He is despised and rejected of men; a man of sorrows, and acquainted with grief: and we hid as it were our faces from him; he was despised, and we esteemed him not.

Isaiah 53:3

He came unto his own, and his own received him not.

John 1:11

For neither did his brethren believe in him.

John 7:5

Have any of the rulers or of the Pharisees believed on him?

John 7:48

And all they in the synagogue, when they heard these things, were filled with wrath,

And rose up, and thrust him out of the city, and led him unto the brow of the hill whereon their city was built, that they might cast him down headlong.

But he passing through the midst of them went his way.

Luke 4:28-30

*   *   *   *

Let not them that are mine enemies wrongfully rejoice over me: neither let them wink with the eye that hate me without a cause.

Psalm 35:19

They that hate me without a cause are more than the hairs of mine head: they that would destroy me, being mine enemies wrongfully, are mighty: then I restored that which I took not away.

Psalm 69:4

For the mouth of the wicked and the mouth of the deceitful are opened against me: they have spoken against me with a lying tongue.

They compassed me about also with words of hatred; and fought against me without a cause.

For my love they are my adversaries: but I give myself unto prayer.

And they have rewarded me evil for good, and hatred for my love.

Psalms 109:2-5

If I had not done among them the works which none other man did, they had not had sin: but now have they both seen and hated both me and my Father.

But this cometh to pass, that the word might be fulfilled that is written in their law, They hated me without a cause.

John 15:24, 25

*   *   *   *

The stone which the builders refused is become the head stone of the corner.

Psalm 118:22

And he beheld them, and said, What is this then that is written, The stone which the builders rejected, the same is become the head of the corner?

Whosoever shall fall upon that stone shall be broken; but on whomsoever it shall fall, it will grind him to powder.

And the chief priests and the scribes the same hour sought to lay hands on him; and they feared the people: for they perceived that he had spoken this parable against them.

Luke 20:17-19

This is the stone which was set at nought of you builders, which is become the head of the corner.

Acts 4:11

And are built upon the foundation of the apostles and prophets, Jesus Christ himself being the chief corner stone.

Ephesians 2:20

* * * *

And he shall be for a sanctuary; but for a stone of stumbling and for a rock of offence to both the houses of Israel, for a gin and for a snare to the inhabitants of Jerusalem.

Isaiah 8:14

Therefore thus saith the LORD God, Behold, I lay in Zion for a foundation a stone, a tried stone, a precious corner stone, a sure foundation: he that believeth shall not make haste.

Isaiah 28:16

Unto you therefore which believe he is precious: but unto them which be disobedient, the stone which the builders disallowed, the same is made the head of the corner.

1 Peter 2:7

Wherefore? Because they sought it not by faith, but as it were by the works of the law. For they stumbled at that stumblingstone;

As it is written, Behold, I lay in Sion a stumblingstone and rock of offence: and whosoever believeth on him shall not be ashamed.

Romans 9:32, 33

* * * *

Thus saith the LORD, the Redeemer of Israel, and his Holy One, to him whom man despiseth, to him whom the

44

nation abhorreth, to a servant of rulers, Kings shall see and arise, princes also shall worship, because of the LORD that is faithful, and the Holy One of Israel, and he shall choose thee.

Isaiah 49:7

And many lepers were in Israel in the time of Eliseus the prophet; and none of them was cleansed, saving Naaman the Syrian.

And all they in the synagogue, when they heard these things, were filled with wrath,

And rose up, and thrust him out of the city, and led him unto the brow of the hill whereon their city was built, that they might cast him down headlong.

But he passing through the midst of them went his way.

Luke 4:27-30

* * * *

I am become a stranger unto my brethren, and an alien unto my mother's children.

Psalm 69:8

He came unto his own, and his own received him not.

John 1:11

His brethren therefore said unto him, Depart hence, and go into Judaea, that thy disciples also may see the works that thou doest.

For there is no man that doeth any thing in secret, and he himself seeketh to be known openly. If thou do these things, shew thyself to the world.

For neither did his brethren believe in him.

John 7:3-5

And he went out from thence, and came into his own country; and his disciples follow him.

And when the sabbath day was come, he began to teach in the synagogue: and many hearing him were astonished, saying, From whence hath this man these things? and what wisdom is this which is given unto him, that even such mighty works are wrought by his hands?

Is not this the carpenter, the son of Mary, the brother of James, and Joses, and of Juda, and Simon? and are not his sisters here with us? And they were offended at him.

Mark 6:1-3

*　*　*　*

Why do the heathen rage, and the people imagine a vain thing?

The kings of the earth set themselves, and the rulers take counsel together, against the LORD, and against his anointed. . .

Psalm 2:1, 2

Then saith he to the man, Stretch forth thine hand. And he stretched it forth; and it was restored whole, like as the other.

Then the Pharisees went out, and held a council against him, how they might destroy him.

Matthew 12:13, 14

Then assembled together the chief priests, and the scribes, and the elders of the people, unto the palace of the high priest, who was called Caiaphas,

And consulted that they might take Jesus by subtilty, and kill him.

But they said, Not on the feast day, lest there be an uproar among the people.

Matthew 26:3-5

*　*　*　*

Many bulls have compassed me: strong bulls of Bashan have beset me round.

Psalm 22:12

After these things Jesus walked in Galilee: for he would not walk in Jewry, because the Jews sought to kill him. . .

The world cannot hate you; but me it hateth, because I testify of it, that the works thereof are evil. . .

Then they sought to take him: but no man laid hands on him; because his hour was not yet come.

And many of the people believed on him, and said, When Christ cometh, will he do more miracles than these which this man hath done?

The Pharisees heard that the people murmured such things concerning him; and the Pharisees and the chief priests sent officers to take him.

John 7:1, 7, 30-32

* * * *

Mine enemies speak evil of me, When shall he die, and his name perish?

Psalm 41:5

Every day they wrest my words: all their thoughts are against me for evil.

Psalm 56:5

And he taught daily in the temple. But the chief priests and the scribes and the chief of the people sought to destroy him,

And could not find what they might do: for all the people were very attentive to hear him.

Luke 19:47, 48

Then gathered the chief priests and the Pharisees a council, and said, What do we? for this man doeth many miracles.

If we let him thus alone, all men will believe on him: and the Romans shall come and take away both our place and nation.

And one of them, named Caiaphas, being the high priest that same year, said unto them, Ye know nothing at all,

Nor consider that it is expedient for us, that one man should die for the people, and that the whole nation perish not.

And this spake he not of himself: but being high priest that year, he prophesied that Jesus should die for that nation;

And not for that nation only, but that also he should gather together in one the children of God that were scattered abroad.

Then from that day forth they took counsel together for to put him to death.

John 11:47-53

47

Now the feast of unleavened bread drew nigh, which is called the Passover.

And the chief priests and scribes sought how they might kill him; for they feared the people.

Luke 22:1, 2

* * * *

And he said, Go, and tell this people, Hear ye indeed, but understand not; and see ye indeed, but perceive not.

Make the heart of this people fat, and make their ears heavy, and shut their eyes; lest they see with their eyes, and hear with their ears, and understand with their heart, and convert, and be healed.

Isaiah 6:9, 10

Who hath believed our report? and to whom is the arm of the LORD revealed?

Isaiah 53:1

I have spread out my hands all the day unto a rebellious people, which walketh in a way that was not good, after their own thoughts.

Isaiah 65:2

And in them is fulfilled the prophecy of Esaias, which saith, By hearing ye shall hear, and shall not understand; and seeing ye shall see, and shall not perceive:

For this people's heart is waxed gross, and their ears are dull of hearing, and their eyes they have closed; lest at any time they should see with their eyes, and hear with their ears, and should understand with their heart, and should be converted, and I should heal them.

But blessed are your eyes, for they see: and your ears, for they hear.

For verily I say unto you, That many prophets and righteous men have desired to see those things which ye see, and have not seen them; and to hear those things which ye hear, and have not heard them.

Matthew 13:14-17

* * * *

Thus saith the LORD, the Redeemer of Israel, and his Holy One, to him whom man despiseth, to him whom the nation abhorreth, to a servant of rulers, Kings shall see and arise, princes also shall worship, because of the LORD that is faithful, and the Holy One of Israel, and he shall choose thee.

Isaiah 49:7

And as he said these things unto them, the scribes and the Pharisees began to urge him vehemently, and to provoke him to speak of many things:

Laying wait for him, and seeking to catch something out of his mouth, that they might accuse him.

Luke 11:53, 54

And when they had blindfolded him, they struck him on the face, and asked him, saying, Prophesy, who is it that smote thee?

And many other things blasphemously spake they against him.

Luke 22:64, 65

HIS BETRAYAL

For it was not an enemy that reproached me; then I could have borne it: neither was it he that hated me that did magnify himself against me; then I would have hid myself from him:

But it was thou, a man mine equal, my guide, and mine acquaintance.

We took sweet counsel together, and walked unto the house of God in company.

Psalm 55:12-14

And while he yet spake, lo, Judas, one of the twelve, came, and with him a great multitude with swords and staves, from the chief priests and elders of the people.

And forthwith he came to Jesus, and said, Hail, master; and kissed him.

And Jesus said unto him, Friend, wherefore art thou come? Then came they, and laid hands on Jesus, and took him.

Matthew 26:47, 49, 50

When Jesus had thus said, he was troubled in spirit, and testified, and said, Verily, verily, I say unto you, that one of you shall betray me.

Jesus answered, He it is, to whom I shall give a sop, when I have dipped it. And when he had dipped the sop, he gave it to Judas Iscariot, the son of Simon.

John 13:21, 26

* * * *

Yea, mine own familiar friend, in whom I trusted, which did eat of my bread, hath lifted up his heel against me.

Psalm 41:9

And while he yet spake, behold a multitude, and he that was called Judas, one of the twelve, went before them, and drew near unto Jesus to kiss him.

But Jesus said unto him, Judas, betrayest thou the Son of man with a kiss?

Luke 22:47, 48

* * * *

And I said unto them, If ye think good, give me my price, and if not, forbear. So they weighed for my price thirty pieces of silver.

Zechariah 11:12

Then one of the twelve, called Judas Iscariot, went unto the chief priests,

And said unto them, What will ye give me, and I will deliver him unto you? And they covenanted with him for thirty pieces of silver.

And from that time he sought opportunity to betray him.

Matthew 26:14-16

* * * *

And one shall say unto him, What are these wounds in thine hands? Then he shall answer, Those with which I was wounded in the house of my friends.

Awake, O sword, against my shepherd, and against the man that is my fellow, saith the LORD of hosts: smite the shepherd, and the sheep shall be scattered: and I will turn mine hand upon the little ones.

Zechariah 13:6, 7

And Jesus saith unto them, All ye shall be offended because of me this night: for it is written, I will smite the shepherd, and the sheep shall be scattered.

Mark 14:27

Then saith Jesus unto them, All ye shall be offended because of me this night: for it is written, I will smite the shepherd, and the sheep of the flock shall be scattered abroad.

Matthew 26:31

And they all forsook him, and fled.

Mark 14:50

And the LORD said unto me, Cast it unto the potter: a goodly price that I was prised at of them. And I took the thirty pieces of silver, and cast them to the potter in the house of the LORD.

Zechariah 11:13

Then Judas, which had betrayed him, when he saw that he was condemned, repented himself, and brought again the thirty pieces of silver to the chief priests and elders,

Saying, I have sinned in that I have betrayed the innocent blood. And they said, What is that to us? see thou to that. And he cast down the pieces of silver in the temple, and departed, and went and hanged himself.

Matthew 27:3-5

And the chief priests took the silver pieces, and said, It is not lawful for to put them into the treasury, because it is the price of blood.

And they took counsel, and bought with them the potter's field, to bury strangers in.

Wherefore that field was called, The field of blood, unto this day.

Then was fulfilled that which was spoken by Jeremy the prophet, saying, And they took the thirty pieces of silver, the price of him that was valued, whom they of the children of Israel did value;

And gave them for the potter's field, as the LORD appointed me.

Matthew 27:6-10

* * * *

Let death seize upon them, and let them go down quick into hell: for wickedness is in their dwellings, and among them.

But thou, O God, shalt bring them down into the pit of destruction: bloody and deceitful men shall not live out half their days; but I will trust in thee.

Psalm 55:15, 23

As he loved cursing, so let it come unto him: as he delighted not in blessing, so let it be far from him.

Psalm 109:17

Men and brethren, this scripture must needs have been fulfilled, which the Holy Ghost by the mouth of David spake before concerning Judas, which was guide to them that took Jesus.

For he was numbered with us, and had obtained part of this ministry.

Now this man purchased a field with the reward of iniquity; and falling headlong, he burst asunder in the midst, and all his bowels gushed out.

And it was known unto all the dwellers at Jerusalem; insomuch as that field is called in their proper tongue, Aceldama, that is to say, The field of blood.

Acts 1:16-19

*   *   *   *

When he shall be judged, let him be condemned: and let his prayer become sin.

Let his days be few; and let another take his office.

Psalm 109:7, 8

Let their habitation be desolate; and let none dwell in their tents.

Psalm 69:25

For it is written in the book of Psalms, Let his habitation be desolate, and let no man dwell therein: and his bishoprik let another take.

And they appointed two, Joseph called Barsabas, who was surnamed Justus, and Matthias.

And they prayed, and said, Thou, LORD, which knowest the hearts of all men, shew whether of these two thou hast chosen,

That he may take part of this ministry and apostleship, from which Judas by transgression fell, that he might go to his own place.

And they gave forth their lots; and the lot fell upon Matthias; and he was numbered with the eleven apostles.

Acts 1:20, 23-26

HIS ACCUSAL AND TRIAL

False witnesses did rise up; they laid to my charge things that I knew not.

Psalm 35:11

And there arose certain, and bare false witness against him, saying,

We heard him say, I will destroy this temple that is made with hands, and within three days I will build another made without hands.

But neither so did their witnesses agree together.

But he held his peace, and answered nothing. Again the high priest asked him, and said unto him, Art thou the Christ, the Son of the Blessed?

And Jesus said, I am: and ye shall see the Son of man sitting on the right hand of power, and coming in the clouds of heaven.

Mark 14:57-59, 61, 62

And when Herod saw Jesus, he was exceeding glad: for he was desirous to see him of a long season, because he had heard many things of him; and he hoped to have seen some miracle done by him.

Then he questioned with him in many words; but he answered him nothing.

And the chief priests and scribes stood and vehemently accused him.

Luke 23:8-10

He was oppressed, and he was afflicted, yet he opened not his mouth: he is brought as a lamb to the slaughter, and as a sheep before her shearers is dumb, so he opened not his mouth.

Isaiah 53:7

But I, as a deaf man, heard not; and I was as a dumb man that openeth not his mouth.

Thus I was as a man that heareth not, and in whose mouth are no reproofs.

Psalm 38:13, 14

And Pilate asked him again, saying, Answerest thou nothing? behold how many things they witness against thee.

But Jesus yet answered nothing; so that Pilate marvelled.

Mark 15:4, 5

And when he was accused of the chief priests and elders, he answered nothing.

Then said Pilate unto him, Hearest thou not how many things they witness against thee?

And he answered him to never a word; insomuch that the governor marvelled greatly.

Now at that feast the governor was wont to release unto the people a prisoner, whom they would.

And they had then a notable prisoner, called Barabbas.

Therefore when they were gathered together, Pilate said unto them, Whom will ye that I release unto you? Barabbas, or Jesus which is called Christ?

For he knew that for envy they had delivered him.

When he was set down on the judgment seat, his wife sent unto him, saying, Have thou nothing to do with that just man: for I have suffered many things this day in a dream because of him.

Matthew 27:12-19

Who did no sin, neither was guile found in his mouth:

Who, when he was reviled, reviled not again; when he suffered, he threatened not; but committed himself to him that judgeth righteously.

1 Peter 2:22, 23

* * * *

Deliver me not over unto the will of mine enemies: for false witnesses are risen up against me, and such as breathe out cruelty.

Psalm 27:12

And they that had laid hold on Jesus led him away to Caiaphas the high priest, where the scribes and the elders were assembled.

Now the chief priests, and elders, and all the council,

55

sought false witness against Jesus, to put him to death;

But found none: yea, though many false witnesses came, yet found they none. At the last came two false witnesses,

And said, This fellow said, I am able to destroy the temple of God, and to build it in three days.

And the high priest arose, and said unto him, Answerest thou nothing? what is it which these witness against thee?

But Jesus held his peace. And the high priest answered and said unto him, I adjure thee by the living God, that thou tell us whether thou be the Christ, the Son of God.

Matthew 26:57, 59-63

* * * *

They that hate me without a cause are more than the hairs of mine head: they that would destroy me, being mine enemies wrongfully, are mighty: then I restored that which I took not away.

Psalm 69:4

For the mouth of the wicked and the mouth of the deceitful are opened against me: they have spoken against me with a lying tongue.

They compassed me about also with words of hatred; and fought against me without a cause.

For my love they are my adversaries: but I give myself unto prayer.

And they have rewarded me evil for good, and hatred for my love.

Psalm 109:2-5

Why do the heathen rage, and the people imagine a vain thing?

The kings of the earth set themselves, and the rulers take counsel together, against the LORD, and against his anointed, saying.

Psalm 2:1, 2

If the world hate you, ye know that it hated me before it hated you.

If ye were of the world, the world would love his own:

but because ye are not of the world, but I have chosen you out of the world, therefore the world hateth you.

Remember the word that I said unto you, The servant is not greater than his lord. If they have persecuted me, they will also persecute you; if they have kept my saying, they will keep yours also.

But all these things will they do unto you for my name's sake, because they know not him that sent me.

If I had not come and spoken unto them, they had not had sin: but now they have no cloke for their sin.

He that hateth me hateth my Father also.

If I had not done among them the works which none other man did, they had not had sin but now have they both seen and hated both me and my Father.

John 15:18-24

The kings of the earth stood up, and the rulers were gathered together against the LORD, and against his Christ.

For of a truth against thy holy child Jesus, whom thou hast anointed, both Herod, and Pontius Pilate, with the Gentiles, and the people of Israel, were gathered together,

For to do whatsoever thy hand and thy counsel determined before to be done.

Acts 4:26-28

DETAILS OF HIS DEATH

From the sole of the foot even unto the head there is no soundness in it; but wounds, and bruises, and putrifying sores: they have not been closed, neither bound up, neither mollified with ointment.

Isaiah 1:6

Then did they spit in his face, and buffeted him; and others smote him with the palms of their hands.

Matthew 26:67

* * * *

My God, my God, why hast thou forsaken me? why art thou so far from helping me, and from the words of my roaring?

Psalm 22:1

And about the ninth hour Jesus cried with a loud voice, saying, Eli, Eli, la-ma sa-bach-tha-ni? that is to say, My God, my God, why hast thou forsaken me?

Matthew 27:46

* * * *

My lovers and my friends stand aloof from my sore; and my kinsmen stand afar off.

Psalm 38:11

And all his acquaintance, and the women that followed him from Galilee, stood afar off, beholding these things.

Luke 23:49

There were also women looking on afar off: among whom was Mary Magdalene, and Mary the mother of James the less and of Joses, and Salome.

Mark 15:40

And many women were there beholding afar off, which followed Jesus from Galilee, ministering unto him:

Among which was Mary Magdalene, and Mary the mother

of James and Joses, and the mother of Zebedee's children.

Matthew 27:55, 56

I became also a reproach unto them: when they looked upon me they shaked their heads.

Psalm 109:25

And they that passed by reviled him, wagging their heads.

Matthew 27:39

* * * *

Therefore will I divide him a portion with the great, and he shall divide the spoil with the strong; because he hath poured out his soul unto death: and he was numbered with the transgressors; and he bare the sin of many, and made intercession for the transgressors.

Isaiah 53:12

And the scripture was fulfilled, which saith, And he was numbered with the transgressors.

Mark 15:28

For I say unto you, that this that is written must yet be accomplished in me, And he was reckoned among the transgressors: for the things concerning me have an end.

Then said Jesus, Father, forgive them; for they know not what they do. And they parted his raiment, and cast lots.

Luke 22:37; 23:34

* * * *

They gave me also gall for my meat; and in my thirst they gave me vinegar to drink.

My strength is dried up like a potsherd; and my tongue cleaveth to my jaws; and thou hast brought me into the dust of death.

Psalm 69:21; 22:15

After this, Jesus knowing that all things were now accomplished, that the scripture might be fulfilled, saith, I thirst.

Now there was set a vessel full of vinegar: and they filled a spunge with vinegar, and put it upon hyssop, and put it to his mouth.

John 19:28, 29

They gave him vinegar to drink mingled with gall: and when he had tasted thereof, he would not drink.

And straightway one of them ran, and took a spunge, and filled it with vinegar, and put it on a reed, and gave him to drink.

Matthew 27:34, 48

*   *   *   *

Into thine hand I commit my spirit: thou hast redeemed me, O LORD God of truth.

Psalm 31:5

And when Jesus had cried with a loud voice, he said, Father, into thy hands I commend my spirit: and having said thus, he gave up the ghost.

Luke 23:46

*   *   *   *

They part my garments among them, and cast lots upon my vesture.

Psalm 22:18

Then the soldiers, when they had crucified Jesus, took his garments, and made four parts, to every soldier a part; and also his coat: now the coat was without seam, woven from the top throughout.

They said therefore among themselves, Let us not rend it, but cast lots for it, whose it shall be: that the scripture might be fulfilled, which saith, They parted my raiment among them, and for my vesture they did cast lots. These things therefore the soldiers did.

John 19:23, 24

Then said Jesus, Father, forgive them; for they know not what they do. And they parted his raiment, and cast lots.

Luke 23:34

He keepeth all his bones: not one of them is broken.

Psalm 34:20

And the LORD said unto Moses and Aaron, This is the ordinance of the passover: There shall no stranger eat thereof:

But every man's servant that is bought for money, when thou hast circumcised him, then shall he eat thereof.

A foreigner and an hired servant shall not eat thereof.

In one house it shall be eaten; thou shalt not carry forth aught of the flesh abroad out of the house; neither shall ye break a bone thereof.

Exodus 12:43-46

They shall leave none of it unto the morning, nor break any bone of it: according to all the ordinances of the passover they shall keep it.

Numbers 9:12

Then came the soldiers, and brake the legs of the first, and of the other which was crucified with him.

But when they came to Jesus, and saw that he was dead already, they brake not his legs:

But one of the soldiers with a spear pierced his side, and forthwith came there out blood and water.

And he that saw it bare record, and his record is true: and he knoweth that he saith true, that ye might believe.

For these things were done, that the scripture should be fulfilled, A bone of him shall not be broken.

John 19:32-36

*   *   *   *

And it shall come to pass in that day, saith the LORD God, that I will cause the sun to go down at noon, and I will darken the earth in the clear day.

Amos 8:9

Now from the sixth hour there was darkness over all the land unto the ninth hour.

Matthew 27:45

And one shall say unto him, What are these wounds in thine hands? Then he shall answer, Those with which I was wounded in the house of my friends.

Zechariah 13:6

61

For dogs have compassed me: the assembly of the wicked have inclosed me: they pierced my hands and my feet.

Psalm 22:16

And when they were come to the place, which is called Calvary, there they crucified him, and the malefactors, one on the right hand, and the other on the left.

Luke 23:33

Then saith he to Thomas, Reach hither thy finger, and behold my hands; and reach hither thy hand, and thrust it into my side: and be not faithless, but believing.

John 20:27

* * * *

For my love they are my adversaries: but I give myself unto prayer.

Psalm 109:4

Therefore will I divide him a portion with the great, and he shall divide the spoil with the strong; because he hath poured out his soul unto death: and he was numbered with the transgressors; and he bare the sin of many, and made intercession for the transgressors.

Isaiah 53:12

Then said Jesus, Father, forgive them; for they know not what they do. . .

Luke 23:34

* * * *

. . .He had done no violence, neither was any deceit in his mouth.

Isaiah 53:9

Who did no sin, neither was guile found in his mouth:
Who, when he was reviled, reviled not again; when he suffered, he threatened not; but committed himself to him that judgeth righteously.

1 Peter 2:22, 23

They shall come, and shall declare his righteousness unto a people that shall be born, that he hath done this.

Psalm 22:31

When Jesus therefore had received the vinegar, he said, It is finished: and he bowed his head, and gave up the ghost.

John 19:30

Thou hast made his glory to cease, and cast his throne down to the ground.

The days of his youth hast thou shortened: thou hast covered him with shame. Selah.

How long, LORD? wilt thou hide thyself for ever? shall thy wrath burn like fire?

Psalm 89:44-46

He weakened my strength in the way; he shortened my days.

I said, O my God, take me not away in the midst of my days: thy years are throughout all generations.

Psalm 102:23, 24

He was taken from prison and from judgment: and who shall declare his generation? for he was cut off out of the land of the living: for the transgression of my people was he stricken.

Isaiah 53:8

And Jesus himself began to be about thirty years of age, being (as was supposed) the son of Joseph, which was the son of Heli.

Luke 3:23

I am poured out like water, and all my bones are out of joint: my heart is like wax; it is melted in the midst of my bowels.

Reproach hath broken my heart; and I am full of heaviness: and I looked for some to take pity, but there was none; and for comforters, but I found none.

Psalms 22:14; 69:20

And I will pour upon the house of David, and upon the inhabitants of Jerusalem, the spirit of grace and of supplications: and they shall look upon me whom they have pierced, and they shall mourn for him, as one mourneth for his only son, and shall be in bitterness for him, as one that is in bitterness for his firstborn.

Zechariah 12:10

But one of the soldiers with a spear pierced his side, and forthwith came there out blood and water.

John 19:34

*   *   *   *

And he made his grave with the wicked, and with the rich in his death. . .

Isaiah 53:9

When the even was come, there came a rich man of Arimathaea, named Joseph, who also himself was Jesus' disciple:

He went to Pilate, and begged the body of Jesus. Then Pilate commanded the body to be delivered.

And when Joseph had taken the body, he wrapped it in a clean linen cloth,

And laid it in his own new tomb, which he had hewn out in the rock: and he rolled a great stone to the door of the sepulchre, and departed.

Matthew 27:57-60

HIS RESURRECTION

I have set the LORD always before me: because he is at my right hand, I shall not be moved.

Therefore my heart is glad, and my glory rejoiceth: my flesh also shall rest in hope.

For thou wilt not leave my soul in hell; neither wilt thou suffer thine Holy One to see corruption.

Psalm 16:8-10

O LORD, thou hast brought up my soul from the grave: thou hast kept me alive, that I should not go down to the pit.

But thou, O LORD, be merciful unto me, and raise me up, that I may requite them.

Psalms 30:3; 41:10

And he saith unto them, Be not affrighted: Ye seek Jesus of Nazareth, which was crucified: he is risen; he is not here: behold the place where they laid him.

But go your way, tell his disciples and Peter that he goeth before you into Galilee: there shall ye see him, as he said unto you.

Mark 16:6, 7

Because thou wilt not leave my soul in hell, neither wilt thou suffer thine Holy One to see corruption.

Thou hast made known to me the ways of life; thou shalt make me full of joy with thy countenance.

Men and brethren, let me freely speak unto you of the patriarch David, that he is both dead and buried, and his sepulchre is with us unto this day.

Therefore being a prophet, and knowing that God had sworn with an oath to him, that of the fruit of his loins, according to the flesh, he would raise up Christ to sit on his throne;

He seeing this before spake of the resurrection of Christ, that his soul was not left in hell, neither his flesh did see corruption.

Acts 2:27-31

God hath fulfilled the same unto us their children, in that he hath raised up Jesus again; as it is also written in the second psalm, Thou art my Son, this day have I begotten thee.

And as concerning that he raised him up from the dead, now no more to return to corruption, he said on this wise, I will give you the sure mercies of David.

Wherefore he saith also in another psalm, Thou shalt not suffer thine Holy One to see corruption.

Acts 13:33-35

* * * *

But God will redeem my soul from the power of the grave: for he shall receive me. Selah.

Psalm 49:15

After two days will he revive us: in the third day he will raise us up, and we shall live in his sight.

Hosea 6:2

I shall not die, but live, and declare the works of the LORD.

Psalm 118:17

And the angel answered and said unto the women, Fear not ye: for I know that ye seek Jesus, which was crucified.

He is not here: for he is risen, as he said. Come, see the place where the LORD lay.

Matthew 28:5-7

And as they thus spake, Jesus himself stood in the midst of them, and saith unto them, Peace be unto you.

But they were terrified and affrighted, and supposed that they had seen a spirit.

And he said unto them, Why are ye troubled? and why do thoughts arise in your hearts?

Behold my hands and my feet, that it is I myself: handle me, and see; for a spirit hath not flesh and bones, as ye see me have.

And when he had thus spoken, he shewed them his hands and his feet.

And while they yet believed not for joy, and wondered, he said unto them, Have ye here any meat?

And they gave him a piece of a broiled fish, and of an honeycomb.

And he took it, and did eat before them.

And he said unto them, These are the words which I spake unto you, while I was yet with you, that all things must be fulfilled, which were written in the law of Moses, and in the prophets, and in the psalms, concerning me.

Then opened he their understanding, that they might understand the scriptures.

And said unto them, Thus it is written, and thus it behoved Christ to suffer, and to rise from the dead the third day:

And that repentance and remission of sins should be preached in his name among all nations, beginning at Jerusalem.

And ye are witnesses of these things.

Luke 24:36-48

Then the same day at evening, being the first day of the week, when the doors were shut where the disciples were assembled for fear of the Jews, came Jesus and stood in the midst, and saith unto them, Peace be unto you.

But Thomas, one of the twelve, called Didymus, was not with them when Jesus came.

The other disciples therefore said unto him, We have seen the LORD. But he said unto them, Except I shall see in his hands the print of the nails, and put my finger into the print of the nails, and thrust my hand into his side, I will not believe.

And after eight days again his disciples were within, and Thomas with them: then came Jesus, the doors being shut, and stood in the midst, and said, Peace be unto you.

Then saith he to Thomas, Reach hither thy finger, and behold my hands; and reach hither thy hand, and thrust it into my side: and be not faithless, but believing.

And Thomas answered and said unto him, My LORD and my God.

Jesus saith unto him, Thomas, because thou hast seen me, thou hast believed: blessed are they that have not seen, and yet have believed.

John 20:19, 24-29

And if Christ be not raised, your faith is vain; ye are yet in your sins.

But now is Christ risen from the dead, and become the firstfruits of them that slept.

1 Corinthians 15:17, 20

Who shall change our vile body, that it may be fashioned like unto his glorious body, according to the working whereby he is able even to subdue all things unto himself.

Philippians 3:21

HIS ASCENSION

For thou wilt not leave my soul in hell; neither wilt thou suffer thine Holy One to see corruption.

Thou wilt shew me the path of life: in thy presence is fulness of joy; at thy right hand there are pleasures for evermore.

Psalm 16:10-11

So then after the LORD had spoken unto them, he was received up into heaven, and sat on the right hand of God.

Mark 16:19

Jesus saith unto her, Mary. She turned herself, and saith unto him, Rabboni; which is to say, Master.

Jesus saith unto her, Touch me not; for I am not yet ascended to my Father: but go to my brethren, and say unto them, I ascend unto my Father, and your Father; and to my God, and your God.

John 20:16, 17

And as they went to tell his disciples, behold, Jesus met them, saying, All hail. And they came and held him by the feet, and worshipped him.

Matthew 28:9

And that he was buried, and that he rose again the third day according to the scriptures.

1 Corinthians 15:4

Thou hast ascended on high, thou hast led captivity captive: thou hast received gifts for men; yea, for the rebellious also, that the LORD God might dwell among them.

Psalm 68:18

And he led them out as far as to Bethany, and he lifted up his hands, and blessed them.

And it came to pass, while he blessed them, he was parted from them, and carried up into heaven.

Luke 24:50, 51

And when he had spoken these things, while they beheld, he was taken up; and a cloud received him out of their sight.

And while they looked stedfastly toward heaven as he went up, behold, two men stood by them in white apparel;

Which also said, Ye men of Galilee, why stand ye gazing up into heaven? this same Jesus, which is taken up from you into heaven, shall so come in like manner as ye have seen him go into heaven.

Acts 1:9-11

* * * *

Lift up your heads, O ye gates; and be ye lift up, ye everlasting doors; and the King of glory shall come in.

Who is this King of glory? The LORD strong and mighty, the LORD mighty in battle.

Lift up your heads, O ye gates; even lift them up, ye everlasting doors; and the King of glory shall come in.

Who is this King of glory? The LORD of hosts, he is the King of glory.

Psalm 24:7-10

Wherefore he saith, When he ascended up on high, he led captivity captive, and gave gifts unto men.

Ephesians 4:8

What and if ye shall see the Son of man ascend up where he was before?

John 6:62

Then said Jesus unto them, Yet a little while am I with you, and then I go unto him that sent me.

John 7:33

Little children, yet a little while I am with you. Ye shall seek me: and as I said unto the Jews, Whither I go, ye cannot come; so now I say to you.

John 13:33

Ye have heard how I said unto you, I go away, and come again unto you. If ye loved me, ye would rejoice, because I said, I go unto the Father: for my Father is greater than I.

And now I have told you before it come to pass, that, when it is come, ye might believe.

John 14:28, 29

70

I shall not die, but live, and declare the works of the LORD.

The LORD hath chastened me sore: but he hath not given me over unto death.

Open to me the gates of righteousness: I will go into them, and I will praise the LORD:

This gate of the LORD, into which the righteous shall enter.

Psalm 118:17-20

Seeing then that we have a great high priest, that is passed into the heavens, Jesus the Son of God, let us hold fast our profession.

For Christ is not entered into the holy places made with hands, which are the figures of the true; but into heaven itself, now to appear in the presence of God for us.

Hebrews 4:14; 9:24

HIS KINGDOM

For unto us a child is born, unto us a son is given: and the government shall be upon his shoulder: and his name shall be called Wonderful, Counsellor, The mighty God, The everlasting Father, The Prince of Peace.

Of the increase of his government and peace there shall be no end, upon the throne of David, and upon his kingdom, to order it, and to establish it with judgment and with justice from henceforth even for ever. The zeal of the LORD of hosts will perform this.

Isaiah 9:6, 7

And when thy days be fulfilled, and thou shalt sleep with thy fathers, I will set up thy seed after thee, which shall proceed out of thy bowels, and I will establish his kingdom.

He shall build an house for my name, and I will stablish the throne of his kingdom for ever.

2 Samuel 7:12, 13

And thine house and thy kingdom shall be established for ever before thee: thy throne shall be established for ever.

According to all these words, and according to all this vision, so did Nathan speak unto David.

2 Samuel 7:16, 17

He shall be great, and shall be called the Son of the Highest: and the LORD God shall give unto him the throne of his father David:

And he shall reign over the house of Jacob for ever; and of his kingdom there shall be no end.

Luke 1:32, 33

* * * *

The sceptre shall not depart from Judah, nor a lawgiver from between his feet, until Shiloh come; and unto him shall the gathering of the people be.

Genesis 49:10

And out of his mouth goeth a sharp sword, that with it he should smite the nations: and he shall rule them with a rod of iron: and he treadeth the winepress of the fierceness and wrath of Almighty God.

And he hath on his vesture and on his thigh a name writen, KING OF KINGS, AND LORD OF LORDS.

Revelation 19:15, 16

* * * *

The LORD said unto my LORD, Sit thou at my right hand, until I make thine enemies thy footstool.

Psalm 110:1

Who being the brightness of his glory, and the express image of his person, and upholding all things by the word of his power, when he had by himself purged our sins, sat down on the right hand of the Majesty on high.

Hebrews 1:3

For David is not ascended into the heavens: but he saith himself, The LORD said unto my LORD, Sit thou on my right hand,

Until I make thy foes thy footstool.

Acts 2:34, 35

* * * *

And speak unto him, saying, Thus speaketh the LORD of hosts, saying, Behold the man whose name is The BRANCH; and he shall grow up out of his place, and he shall build the temple of the LORD.

Zechariah 6:12

Rejoice greatly, O daughter of Zion; shout, O daughter of Jerusalem: behold, thy King cometh unto thee: he is just, and having salvation; lowly, and riding upon an ass, and upon a colt the foal of an ass.

And I will cut off the chariot from Ephraim, and the horse from Jerusalem, and the battle bow shall be cut off: and he shall speak peace unto the heathen: and his dominion shall be from sea even to sea, and from the river even to the ends of the earth.

Zechariah 9:9, 10

73

And there was given him dominion, and glory, and a kingdom, that all people, nations, and languages, should serve him: his dominion is an everlasting dominion, which shall not pass away, and his kingdom that which shall not be destroyed.

Daniel 7:14

Saying, Where is he that is born King of the Jews? for we have seen his star in the east, and are come to worship him.

Matthew 2:2

Tell ye the daughter of Sion, Behold, thy King cometh unto thee, meek, and sitting upon an ass, and a colt the foal of an ass.

Matthew 21:5

Then shall the King say unto them on his right hand, Come, ye blessed of my Father, inherit the kingdom prepared for you from the foundation of the world.

Matthew 25: 34

And the seventh angel sounded; and there were great voices in heaven, saying, The kingdoms of this world are become the kingdoms of our LORD, and of his Christ; and he shall reign for ever and ever.

Revelation 11: 15

And I heard a loud voice saying in heaven, Now is come salvation, and strength, and the kingdom of our God, and the power of his Christ: for the accuser of our brethren is cast down, which accused them before our God day and night.

Revelation 12:10

At that time they shall call Jerusalem the throne of the LORD; and all the nations shall be gathered unto it, to the name of the LORD, to Jerusalem: neither shall they walk any more after the imagination of their evil heart.

Jeremiah 3:17

The wolf also shall dwell with the lamb, and the leopard shall lie down with the kid; and the calf and the young lion and the fatling together; and a little child shall lead them.

And the cow and the bear shall feed; their young ones shall lie down together: and the lion shall eat straw like the ox.

And the sucking child shall play on the hole of the asp, and the weaned child shall put his hand on the cockatrice' den.

They shall not hurt nor destroy in all my holy mountain: for the earth shall be full of the knowledge of the LORD, as the waters cover the sea.

And in that day there shall be a root of Jesse, which shall stand for an ensign of the people; to it shall the Gentiles seek: and his rest shall be glorious.

Isaiah 11:6-10

Even them will I bring to my holy mountain, and make them joyful in my house of prayer: their burnt offerings and their sacrifices shall be accepted upon mine altar; for mine house shall be called an house of prayer for all people.

Isaiah 56:7

Behold, the days come, saith the LORD, that I will make a new covenant with the house of Israel, and with the house of Judah:

Not according to the covenant that I made with their fathers in the day that I took them by the hand to bring them out of the land of Egypt; which my covenant they brake, although I was an husband unto them, saith the LORD:

But this shall be the covenant that I will make with the house of Israel; After those days, saith the LORD, I will put my law in their inward parts, and write it in their hearts; and will be their God, and they shall be my people.

And they shall teach no more every man his neighbour, and every man his brother, saying, Know the LORD: for they shall all know me, from the least of them unto the greatest of them, saith the LORD: for I will forgive their iniquity, and I will remember their sin no more.

Jeremiah 31:31-34

For finding fault with them, he saith, Behold, the days come, saith the LORD, when I will make a new covenant with the house of Judah:

Not according to the covenant that I made with their fathers in the day when I took them by the hand to lead them out of the land of Egypt; because they continued not in my covenant, and I regarded them not, saith the LORD.

For this is the covenant that I will make with the house of Israel after those days, saith the LORD; I will put my laws into their mind, and write them in their hearts: and I will be to them a God, and they shall be to me a people:

And they shall not teach every man his neighbour, and every man his brother, saying, Know the LORD: for all shall know me, from the least to the greatest.

For I will be merciful to their unrighteousness, and their sins and their iniquities will I remember no more.

In that he saith, A new covenant, he hath made the first old. Now that which decayeth and waxeth old is ready to vanish away.

Hebrews 8:8-13

For if the blood of bulls and of goats, and the ashes of an heifer sprinkling the unclean, sanctifieth to the purifying of the flesh:

How much more shall the blood of Christ, who through the eternal Spirit offered himself without spot to God, purge your conscience from dead works to serve the living God?

And for this cause he is the mediator of the new testament, that by means of death, for the redemption of the transgressions that were under the first testament, they which are called might receive the promise of eternal inheritance.

And almost all things are by the law purged with blood; and without shedding of blood is no remission.

Hebrews 9:13-15, 22

And so all Israel shall be saved: as it is written, There shall come out of Sion the Deliverer, and shall turn away ungodliness from Jacob:

For this is my covenant unto them, when I shall take away their sins.

Romans 11:26, 27

HIS OBEDIENCE

Sacrifice and offering thou didst not desire; mine ears hast thou opened: burnt offering and sin offering hast thou not required.

Then said I, Lo, I come: in the volume of the book it is written of me,

I delight to do thy will, O my God: yea, thy law is within my heart.

Psalm 40:6-8

Wherefore when he cometh into the world, he saith, Sacrifice and offering thou wouldest not, but a body hast thou prepared me:

In burnt offerings and sacrifices for sin thou hast had no pleasure.

Then said I, Lo, I come (in the volume of the book it is written of me,) to do thy will, O God.

Hebrews 10:5-7

* * * *

The LORD God hath opened mine ear, and I was not rebellious, neither turned away back.

I gave my back to the smiters, and my cheeks to them that plucked off the hair: I hid not my face from shame and spitting.

Isaiah 50:5, 6

And he went a little farther, and fell on his face, and prayed, saying, O my Father, if it be possible, let this cup pass from me: nevertheless not as I will, but as thou wilt.

Matthew 26:39

And being found in fashion as a man, he humbled himself, and became obedient unto death, even the death of the cross.

Philippians 2:8

Though he were a Son, yet learned he obedience by the things which he suffered.

Hebrews 5:8

Above when he said, Sacrifice and offering and burnt offerings and offering for sin thou wouldest not, neither hadst pleasure therein; which are offered by the law;

Then said he, Lo, I come to do thy will, O God. He taketh away the first, that he may establish the second.

Hebrews 10:8, 9

I have glorified thee on the earth: I have finished the work which thou gavest me to do.

John 17:4

SON OF MAN

(Son of Man is a term for the Messiah that is used over 80 times in the Scriptures. Here is a small sampling.)

I will declare the decree: the LORD hath said unto me, Thou art my Son; this day have I begotten thee.

Kiss the Son, lest he be angry, and ye perish from the way, when his wrath is kindled but a little. Blessed are all they that put their trust in him.

Psalm 2:7, 12

God hath fulfilled the same unto us their children, in that he hath raised up Jesus again; as it is also written in the second psalm, Thou art my Son, this day have I begotten thee.

Acts 13:33

And lo a voice from heaven, saying, This is my beloved Son, in whom I am well pleased.

Matthew 3:17

For unto which of the angels said he at any time, Thou art my son, this day have I begotten thee? And again, I will be to him a Father, and he shall be to me a Son?

So also Christ glorified not himself to be made an high priest; but he that said unto him, Thou art my Son, to day have I begotten thee.

Hebrews 1:5; 5:5

And their nobles shall be of themselves, and their governor shall proceed from the midst of them; and I will cause him to draw near, and he shall approach unto me: for who is this that engaged his heart to approach unto me? saith the LORD.

Jeremiah 30:21

And he went out from thence, and came into his own country; and his disciples follow him.

And when the sabbath day was come, he began to teach in the synagogue: and many hearing him were astonished, saying, From whence hath this man these things? and what wisdom is this which is given unto him, that even such mighty works are wrought by his hands?

Is not this the carpenter, the son of Mary, the brother of James, and Joses, and of Juda, and Simon? and are not his sisters here with us? And they were offended at him.

But Jesus said unto them, A prophet is not without honour, but in his own country, and among his own kin, and in his own house.

Mark 6:1-4

* * * *

And he said unto me, Son of man, stand upon thy feet, and I will speak unto thee.

And the spirit entered into me when he spake unto me, and set me upon my feet, that I heard him that spake unto me.

And he said unto me, Son of man, I send thee to the children of Israel, to a rebellious nation that hath rebelled against me: they and their fathers have transgressed against me, even unto this very day.

For they are impudent children and stiffhearted. I do send thee unto them; and thou shalt say unto them, Thus saith the LORD God.

And they, whether they will hear, or whether they will forbear, (for they are a rebellious house,) yet shall know that there hath been a prophet among them.

And thou, son of man, be not afraid of them, neither be afraid of their words, though briers and thorns be with thee, and thou dost dwell among scorpions: be not afraid of their words, nor be dismayed at their looks, though they be a rebellious house.

And thou shalt speak my words unto them, whether they will hear, or whether they will forbear: for they are most rebellious.

But thou, son of man, hear what I say unto thee; Be not thou rebellious like that rebellious house: open thy mouth, and eat that I give thee.

And when I looked, behold, an hand was sent unto me; and, lo, a roll of a book was therein;

And he spread it before me; and it was written within and

without: and there was written therein lamentations, and mourning, and woe.

Ezekiel 2:1-10

And Jesus saith unto him, The foxes have holes, and the birds of the air have nests; but the Son of man hath not where to lay his head.

Matthew 8:20

But that ye may know that the Son of man hath power on earth to forgive sins, (then saith he to the sick of the palsy,) Arise, take up thy bed, and go unto thine house.

Matthew 9:6

But when they persecute you in this city, flee ye into another: for verily I say unto you, Ye shall not have gone over the cities of Israel, till the Son of man be come.

Matthew 10:23

The Son of man came eating and drinking, and they say, Behold a man gluttonous, and a winebibber, a friend of publicans and sinners. But wisdom is justified of her children.

Matthew 11:19

For the Son of man is LORD even of the sabbath day.

Matthew 12:8

For as Jonas was three days and three nights in the whale's belly; so shall the Son of man be three days and three nights in the heart of the earth.

Matthew 12:40

When Jesus came into the coasts of Caesarea Philippi, he asked his disciples, saying, Whom do men say that I the Son of man am?

And they said, Some say that thou art John the Baptist: some, Elias; and others, Jeremias, or one of the prophets.

He saith unto them, But whom say ye that I am?

And Simon Peter answered and said, Thou art the Christ, the Son of the living God.

Matthew 16:13-16

Whosoever therefore shall be ashamed of me and of my words in this adulterous and sinful generation; of him also shall the Son of man be ashamed, when he cometh in the glory of his Father with the holy angels.

Mark 8:38

But he, being full of the Holy Ghost, looked up stedfastly into heaven, and saw the glory of God, and Jesus standing on the right hand of God,

And said, Behold, I see the heavens opened, and the Son of man standing on the right hand of God.

Acts 7:55, 56

And in the midst of the seven candlesticks one like unto the Son of man, clothed with a garment down to the foot, and girt about the paps with a golden girdle.

Revelation 1:13

HIS GODLY ATTRIBUTES

But thou, Beth-lehem Ephratah, though thou be little among the thousands of Judah, yet out of thee shall he come forth unto me that is to be ruler in Israel; whose goings forth have been from of old, from everlasting.

Micah 5:2

In the beginning was the Word, and the Word was with God, and the Word was God.

John 1:1

Saying, I am Alpha and Omega, the first and the last: and, What thou seest, write in a book, and send it unto the seven churches which are in Asia; unto Ephesus, and unto Smyrna, and unto Pergamos, and unto Thyatira, and unto Sardis, and unto Philadelphia, and unto Laodicea.

Revelation 1:11

*   *   *   *

In the year that king Uzziah died I saw also the LORD sitting upon a throne, high and lifted up, and his train filled the temple.

Above it stood the seraphims: each one had six wings; with twain he covered his face, and with twain he covered his feet, and with twain he did fly.

And one cried unto another, and said, Holy, holy, holy, is the LORD of hosts: the whole earth is full of his glory.

Isaiah 6:1-3

These things said Esaias, when he saw his glory, and spake of him.

John 12:41

*   *   *   *

And the spirit of the LORD shall rest upon him, the spirit of wisdom and understanding, the spirit of counsel and might, the spirit of knowledge and of the fear of the LORD.

Isaiah 11:2

And Jesus, when he was baptized, went up straightway out of the water: and, lo, the heavens were opened unto him, and he saw the Spirit of God descending like a dove, and lighting upon him.

Matthew 3:16

And John bare record, saying, I saw the Spirit descending from heaven like a dove, and it abode upon him.

John 1:32

Howbeit when he, the Spirit of truth, is come, he will guide you into all truth: for he shall not speak of himself; but whatsoever he shall hear, that shall he speak: and he will shew you things to come.

John 16:13

But of him are ye in Christ Jesus, who of God is made unto us wisdom, and righteousness, and sanctification, and re demption.

1 Corninthians 1:30

That the God of our LORD Jesus Christ, the Father of glory, may give unto you the spirit of wisdom and revelation in the knowledge of him:

The eyes of your understanding being enlightened; that ye may know what is the hope of his calling, and what the riches of the glory of his inheritance in the saints.

Ephesians 1:17, 18

For God hath not given us the spirit of fear; but of power, and of love, and of a sound mind.

2 Timothy 1:7

And when he was come into his own country, he taught them in their synagogue, insomuch that they were astonished, and said, Whence hath this man this wisdom, and these mighty works?

Matthew 13:54

And the child grew, and waxed strong in spirit, filled with wisdom: and the grace of God was upon him.

And Jesus increased in wisdom and stature, and in favour with God and man.

Luke 2:40, 52

OTHER ATTRIBUTES OF GOD
THAT JESUS DEMONSTRATED

1. Omnipotence (all-powerful)

And Jesus came and spake unto them, saying, All power is given unto me in heaven and in earth.

Matthew 28:18

2. Omiscient (all-knowing)

And needed not that any should testify of man: for he knew what was in man.

John 2:25

And immediately when Jesus perceived in his spirit that they so reasoned within themselves, he said unto them, Why reason ye these things in your hearts?

Mark 2:8

3. Omnipresent (all-present)

Teaching them to observe all things whatsoever I have commanded you: and, lo, I am with you alway, even unto the end of the world. Amen.

Matthew 28:20

HIS PERFECTION

Thou art fairer than the children of men: grace is poured into thy lips: therefore God hath blessed thee for ever.

Psalm 45:2

For we have not an high priest which cannot be touched with the feeling of our infirmities; but was in all points tempted like as we are, yet without sin.

Hebrews 4:15

Who did no sin, neither was guile found in his mouth.

1 Peter 2:22

* * * *

And therefore will the LORD wait, that he may be gracious unto you, and therefore will he be exalted, that he may have mercy upon you: for the LORD is a God of judgment: blessed are all they that wait for him.

For the people shall dwell in Zion at Jerusalem: thou shalt weep no more: he will be very gracious unto thee at the voice of thy cry; when he shall hear it, he will answer thee.

Isaiah 30:18, 19

Being forty days tempted of the devil. And in those days he did eat nothing: and when they were ended, he afterward hungered.

Luke 4:2

The officers answered, Never man spake like this man.

John 7:46

* * * *

And he made his grave with the wicked, and with the rich in his death; because he had done no violence, neither was any deceit in his mouth.

Isaiah 53:9

And we indeed justly; for we receive the due reward of our deeds: but this man hath done nothing amiss.

Luke 23:41

And though they found no cause of death in him, yet desired they Pilate that he should be slain.

Acts 13:28

For he hath made him to be sin for us, who knew no sin; that we might be made the righteousness of God in him.

2 Corinthians 5:21

But with the precious blood of Christ, as of a lamb without blemish and without spot.

1 Peter 1:19

And ye know that he was manifested to take away our sins; and in him is no sin.

1 John 3:5

How much more shall the blood of Christ, who through the eternal Spirit offered himself without spot to God, purge your conscience from dead works to serve the living God?

Hebrews 9:14

For it became him, for whom are all things, and by whom are all things, in bringing many sons unto glory, to make the captain of their salvation perfect through sufferings.

Hebrews 2:10

For such an high priest became us, who is holy, harmless, undefiled, seperate from sinners, and made higher than the heavens;
For the law maketh men high priests which have infirmity; but the word of the oath, which was since the law, maketh the Son, who is consecrated for evermore.

Hebrews 7:26, 28

And being made perfect, he became the author of eternal salvation unto all them that obey him.

Hebrews 5:9

*   *   *   *

And he shall stand and feed in the strength of the LORD, in the majesty of the name of the LORD his God; and they shall abide: for now shall he be great unto the ends of the earth.

Micah 5:4

When Pilate saw that he could prevail nothing, but that rather a tumult was made, he took water, and washed his hands before the multitude, saying, I am innocent of the blood of this just person: see ye to it.

Matthew 27:24

Pilate therefore went forth again, and saith unto them, Behold, I bring him forth to you, that ye may know that I find no fault in him.

John 19:4

HE IS OUR SHEPHERD

But his bow abode in strength, and the arms of his hands were made strong by the hands of the mighty God of Jacob; (from thence is the Shepherd, the stone of Israel:).

Genesis 49:24

And when the chief Shepherd shall appear, ye shall receive a crown of glory that fadeth not away.

1 Peter 5:4

*   *   *   *

He shall feed his flock like a shepherd: he shall gather the lambs with his arm, and carry them in his bosom, and shall gently lead those that are with young.

Isaiah 40:11

For the Son of man is come to save that which was lost.

How think ye? if a man have an hundred sheep, and one of them be gone astray, doth he not leave the ninety and nine, and goeth into the mountains, and seeketh that which is gone astray?

And if so be that he find it, verily I say unto you, he rejoiceth more of that sheep, than of the ninety and nine which went not astray.

Matthew 18:11-13

And I will set up one shepherd over them, and he shall feed them, even my servant David; he shall feed them, and he shall be their shepherd.

Ezekiel 34:23

And I will raise up for them a plant of renown, and they shall be no more consumed with hunger in the land, neither bear the shame of the heathen any more.

Thus shall they know that I the LORD their God am with them, and that they, even the house of Israel, are my people, saith the Lord God.

And ye my flock, the flock of my pasture, are men, and I am your God, saith the LORD God.

Ezekiel 34:29-31

And David my servant shall be king over them; and they all shall have one shepherd. they shall also walk in my judgments, and observe my statutes, and do them.

Ezekiel 37:24

And he shall stand and feed in the strength of the LORD, in the majesty of the name of the LORD his God; and they shall abide: for now shall he be great unto the ends of the earth.

Micah 5:4

But Jesus said unto them, A prophet is not without honour, but in his own country, and among his own kin, and in his own house.

Mark 6:4

But when he saw the multitudes, he was moved with compassion on them, because they fainted, and were scattered abroad, as sheep having no shepherd.

Matthew 9:36

Now the God of peace, that brought again from the dead our LORD Jesus, that great shepherd of the sheep, through the blood of the everlasting covenant.

Hebrews 13:20

* * * *

He shall feed his flock like a shepherd: he shall gather the lambs with his arm, and carry them in his bosom, and shall gently lead those that are with young.

Isaiah 40:11

I am the good shepherd, and know my sheep, and am known of mine.

As the Father knoweth me, even so know I the Father: and I lay down my life for the sheep.

And other sheep I have, which are not of this fold: them also I must bring, and they shall hear my voice; and there shall be one fold, and one shepherd.

John 10:14-16

He restoreth my soul: he leadeth me in the paths of righteousness for his name's sake.

Psalm 23:3

Behold, the LORD God will come with strong hand, and his arm shall rule for him: behold, his reward is with him, and his work before him.

He shall feed his flock like a shepherd: he shall gather the lambs with his arm, and carry them in his bosom, and shall gently lead those that are with young.

Isaiah 40:10, 11

I am the door: by me if any man enter in, he shall be saved, and shall go in and out, and find pasture.

John 10:9

* * * *

Awake, O sword, against my shepherd, and against the man that is my fellow, saith the LORD of hosts: smite the shepherd, and the sheep shall be scattered: and I will turn mine hand upon the little ones.

Zechariah 13:7

Then saith Jesus unto them, All ye shall be offended because of me this night: for it is written, I will smite the shepherd, and the sheep of the flock shall be scattered abroad.

Matthew 26:31

Take heed therefore unto yourselves, and to all the flock, over the which the Holy Ghost hath made you overseers, to feed the church of God, which he hath purchased with his own blood.

Acts 20:28

* * * *

Hear the word of the LORD, O ye nations, and declare it in the isles afar off, and say, He that scattered Israel will gather him, and keep him, as a shepherd doth his flock.

Jeremiah 31:10

Thus saith the LORD God; Behold, I am against the shepherds; and I will require my flock at their hand, and cause them to cease from feeding the flock; neither shall the shepherds feed themselves any more; for I will deliver my flock from their mouth, that they may not be meat for them.

Ezekiel 34:10

And the LORD their God shall save them in that day as the flock of his people: for they shall be as the stones of a crown, lifted up as an ensign upon his land.

Zechariah 9:16

And I give unto them eternal life; and they shall never perish, neither shall any man pluck them out of my hand.

John 10:28

For thus saith the LORD God; Behold, I, even I, will both search my sheep, and seek them out.

As a shepherd seeketh out his flock in the day that he is among his sheep that are scattered; so will I seek out my sheep, and will deliver them out of all places where they have been scattered in the cloudy and dark day.

Seemeth it a small thing unto you to have eaten up the good pasture, but ye must tread down with your feet the residue of your pastures? and to have drunk of the deep waters, but ye must foul the residue with your feet?

Ezekiel 34:11, 12, 18

For the Son of man is come to seek and to save that which was lost.

Luke 19:10

HIS AUTHORITY

For the zeal of thine house hath eaten me up; and the reproaches of them that reproached thee are fallen upon me.

Psalm 69:9

And when he had made a scourge of small cords, he drove them all out of the temple, and the sheep, and the oxen; and poured out the changers' money, and overthrew the tables;

And said unto them that sold doves, Take these things hence; make not my Father's house an house of merchandise.

And his disciples remembered that it was written, The zeal of thine house hath eaten me up.

John 2:15-17

*　*　*　*

And I will cut off the chariot from Ephraim, and the horse from Jerusalem, and the battle bow shall be cut off: and he shall speak peace unto the heathen: and his dominion shall be from sea even to sea, and from the river even to the ends of the earth.

Zechariah 9:10

But the men marvelled, saying, What manner of man is this, that even the winds and the sea obey him!

Matthew 8:27

For he taught them as one having authority, and not as the scribes.

Matthew 7:29

And Jesus came and spake unto them, saying, All power is given unto me in heaven and in earth.

Matthew 28:18

For the Father judgeth no man, but hath committed all judgment unto the Son:

And hath given him authority to execute judgment also, because he is the Son of man.

John 5:22, 27

*　*　*　*

I the LORD search the heart, I try the reins, even to give every man according to his ways, and according to the fruit of his doings.

Jeremiah 17:10

And Jesus said, I am: and ye shall see the Son of man sitting on the right hand of power, and coming in the clouds of heaven.

Mark 14:62

HIS SPECIAL REVELATION

I will raise them up a Prophet from among their brethren, like unto thee, and will put my words in his mouth; and he shall speak unto them all that I shall command him.

Deuteronomy 18:18

And the multitude said, This is Jesus the prophet of Nazareth of Galilee.

Matthew 21:11

And there came a fear on all: and they glorified God, saying, That a great prophet is risen up among us; and, That God hath visited his people.

Luke 7:16

The woman saith unto him, Sir, I perceive that thou art a prophet.

John 4:19

Then those men, when they had seen the miracle that Jesus did, said, This is of a truth that prophet that should come into the world.

John 6:14

Many of the people therefore, when they heard this saying, said, Of a truth this is the Prophet.

John 7:40

I will open my mouth in a parable: I will utter dark sayings of old.

Psalm 78:2

All these things spake Jesus unto the multitude in parables; and without a parable spake he not unto them.

Matthew 13:34

* * * *

And the Gentiles shall come to thy light, and kings to the brightness of thy rising.

And he said, It is a light thing that thou shouldest be my servant to raise up the tribes of Jacob, and to restore the preserved of Israel: I will also give thee for a light to the Gentiles, that thou mayest be my salvation unto the end of the earth.

Isaiah 60:3; 49:6

For so hath the LORD commanded us, saying, I have set thee to be a light of the Gentiles, that thou shouldest be for salvation unto the ends of the earth.

And when the Gentiles heard this, they were glad, and glorified the word of the LORD: and as many as were ordained to eternal life believed.

Acts 13:47, 48

That Christ should suffer, and that he should be the first that should rise from the dead, and should shew light unto the people, and to the Gentiles.

Acts 26:23

Be it known therefore unto you, that the salvation of God is sent unto the Gentiles, and that they will hear it.

Acts 28:28

* * * *

HIS OMNIPOTENCE
(He is All-Powerful)

Thy people shall be willing in the day of thy power, in the beauties of holiness from the womb of the morning: thou hast the dew of thy youth.

Psalm 110:3

The LORD is slow to anger, and great in power, and will not at all acquit the wicked: the LORD hath his way in the whirlwind and in the storm, and the clouds are the dust of his feet.

Nahum 1:3

And he stood over her, and rebuked the fever; and it left her: and immediately she arose and ministered unto them.

Luke 4:39

And he came and touched the bier: and they that bare him stood still. And he said, Young man, I say unto thee, Arise.

And he that was dead sat up, and began to speak. And he delivered him to his mother.

Luke 7:14, 15

And he put them all out, and took her by the hand, and called, saying, Maid, arise.

And her spirit came again, and she arose straightway: and he commanded to give her meat.

Luke 8:54, 55

Behold, the LORD God will come with strong hand, and his arm shall rule for him: behold, his reward is with him, and his work before him.

Isaiah 40:10

Which he wrought in Christ, when he raised him from the dead, and set him at his own right hand in the heavenly places,

Far above all principality, and power, and might, and dominion, and every name that is named, not only in this world, but also in that which is to come:

And hath put all things under his feet, and gave him to be head over all things to the church,

Which is his body, the fulness of him that filleth all in all.

Ephesians 1:20-23

Wherefore, when I came, was there no man? when I called, was there none to answer? Is my hand shortened at all, that it cannot redeem? or have I no power to deliver? behold, at my rebuke I dry up the sea, I make the rivers a wilderness: their fish stinketh, because there is no water, and dieth for thirst.

I clothe the heavens with blackness, and I make sackcloth their covering.

Isaiah 50:2, 3

And Jesus came and spake unto them, saying, All power is given unto me in heaven and in earth.

Matthew 28:18

* * * *

I know that thou canst do every thing, and that no thought can be withholden from thee.

Job 42:2

Is any thing too hard for the LORD? At the time appointed I will return unto thee, according to the time of life, and Sarah shall have a son.

Genesis 18:14

But Jesus beheld them, and said unto them, With men this is impossible; but with God all things are possible.

Matthew 19:26

* * * *

For he commandeth, and raiseth the stormy wind, which lifteth up the waves thereof.

Psalm 107:25

And he saith unto them, Why are ye fearful, O ye of little faith? Then he arose, and rebuked the winds and the sea; and there was a great calm.

But the men marvelled, saying, What manner of man is this, that even the winds and the sea obey him!

And when he was come to the other side into the country of the Gergesenes, there met him two possessed with devils, coming out of the tombs, exceeding fierce, so that no man might pass by that way.

And, behold, they cried out, saying, What have we to do with thee, Jesus, thou Son of God? art thou come hither to torment us before the time?

Matthew 8:26-29

HIS OMNISCIENCE
(He Knows All)

Counsel is mine, and sound wisdom: I am understanding; I have strength.

Proverbs 8:14

And the spirit of the LORD shall rest upon him, the spirit of wisdom and understanding, the spirit of counsel and might, the spirit of knowledge and the fear of the LORD.

Isaiah 11:2

And Jesus knowing their thoughts said, Wherefore think ye evil in your hearts?

Matthew 9:4

And Jesus knew their thoughts, and said unto them, Every kingdom divided against itself is brought to desolation; and every city or house divided against itself shall not stand.

Matthew 12:25

But he knew their thoughts, and said to the man which had the withered hand, Rise up, and stand forth in the midst. And he arose and stood forth.

Luke 6:8

And he said unto them, Behold, when ye are entered into the city, there shall a man meet you, bearing a pitcher of water; follow him into the house where he entereth in.

And ye shall say unto the goodman of the house, The Master saith unto thee, Where is the guestchamber, where I shall eat the passover with my disciples?

And he shall shew you a large upper room furnished: there make ready.

And they went, and found as he had said unto them: and they made ready the passover.

Luke 22:10-13

But there are some of you that believe not. For Jesus knew from the beginning who they were that believed not, and who should betray him.

John 6:64

Jesus therefore, knowing all things that should come upon him, went forth, and said unto them, Whom seek ye?

John 18:4

* * * *

Dost thou know the balancings of the clouds, the wondrous works of him which is perfect in knowledge?

Job 37:16

For if our heart condemn us, God is greater than our heart, and knoweth all things.

1 John 3:20

* * * *

I will speak of the glorious honour of thy majesty, and of thy wondrous works.

Psalm 145:5

In whom are hid all the treasures of wisdom and knowledge.

Colossians 2:3

* * * *

The eyes of the LORD are in every place, beholding the evil and the good.

Proverbs 15:3

Nathanael saith unto him, Whence knowest thou me? Jesus answered and said unto him, Before that Philip called thee, when thou wast under the fig tree, I saw thee.

John 1:48

* * * *

Thou knowest my downsitting and mine uprising, thou understandest my thought afar off.

Thou compassest my path and my lying down, and art acquainted with all my ways.

For there is not a word in my tongue, but, lo, O LORD, thou knowest it altogether.

Psalm 139:2-4

Jesus saith unto her, Go, call thy husband, and come hither.

The woman answered and said, I have no husband. Jesus said unto her, Thou hast well said, I have no husband:

For thou hast had five husbands; and he whom thou now hast is not thy husband: in that saidst thou truly.

The woman saith unto him, Sir, I perceive that thou art a prophet.

The woman then left her waterpot, and went her way into the city, and saith to the men,

Come, see a man, which told me all things that I ever did: is not this the Christ?

John 4:16-19, 28, 29

* * * *

The heart is deceitful above all things, and desperately wicked: who can know it?

I the LORD search the heart, I try the reins, even to give every man according to his ways, and according to the fruit of his doings.

Jeremiah 17:9, 10

But Jesus did not commit himself unto them, because he knew all men,

And needed not that any should testify of man: for he knew what was in man.

John 2:24, 25

HIS OMNIPRESENCE

Whither shall I go from thy spirit? or whither shall I flee from thy presence?

If I ascend up into heaven, thou art there: if I make my bed in hell, behold, thou art there.

If I take the wings of the morning, and dwell in the uttermost parts of the sea;

Even there shall thy hand lead me, and thy right hand shall hold me.

Psalm 139:7-10

For where two or three are gathered together in my name, there am I in the midst of them.

Matthew 18:20

*   *   *   *

Am I a God at hand, saith the LORD, and not a God afar off?

Can any hide himself in secret places that I shall not see him? saith the LORD. Do not I fill heaven and earth? saith the LORD.

Jeremiah 23:23, 24

Teaching them to observe all things whatsoever I have commanded you: and, lo, I am with you alway, even unto the end of the world. Amen.

Matthew 28:20

And I John saw the holy city, new Jerusalem, coming down from God out of heaven, prepared as a bride adorned for her husband.

And I heard a great voice out of heaven saying, Behold, the tabernacle of God is with men, and he will dwell with them, and they shall be his people, and God himself shall be with them, and be their God.

And he carried me away in the spirit to a great and high mountain, and shewed me that great city, the holy Jerusalem, descending out of heaven from God,

And I saw no temple therein: for the LORD God Almighty and the Lamb are the temple of it.

And the city had no need of the sun, neither of the moon, to shine in it: for the glory of God did lighten it, and the Lamb is the light thereof.

Revelation 21:2, 3, 10, 22, 23

* * * *

But thou, Beth-lehem Ephratah, though thou be little among the thousands of Judah, yet out of thee shall he come forth unto me that is to be ruler in Israel; whose goings forth have been from of old, from everlasting.

Micah 5:2

At that day ye shall know that I am in my Father, and ye in me, and I in you.

John 14:20

In the beginning was the Word, and the Word was with God, and the Word was God.

John 1:1

And he is before all things, and by him all things consist.

Colossians 1:17

HIS NAMES AND TITLES

1. The Amen .... Revelation 3:14
2. Angel .... Genesis 48:16;
   Exodus 23:20, 21
3. Anointed .... Psalm 2:2
4. Apostle .... Hebrews 3:1
5. Author & Finisher
   of our Faith .... Hebrews 12:2
6. Beginning & End of the
   Creation of God................... Revelation 22:13; 3:14
7. Beloved Son .... Matthew 3:17
8. My Beloved .... Ephesians 1:6
9. Only Begotten .... John 1:14; 1:18
10. The Branch .... Isaiah 11:1;
    Matthew 2:23
11. Bread of Life .... John 6:32
12. Bridegroom .... Matthew 9:15
13. Christ, "Messiah, the Anointed
    One" .... John 1:41
14. Consolation .... Luke 2:25
15. Cornerstone .... Ephesians 2:20
16. Counselor........................ Isaiah 9:6;
    Colossians 2:3
17. Dayspring........................ Luke 1:78
18. Deliverer........................ Luke 2:11
19. Door............................. John 10:9
20. Emmanual .... Isaiah 7:14
21. The Faithful Witness .... Revelation 5:5
22. The Father of Eternity .... Isaiah 9:6;
    Revelation 1:8
23. God .... Isaiah 9:6; John 1:1
24. God, My Saviour .... Isaiah 45:15
25. The Mighty God .... Isaiah 9:6; John 1:1-3
26. Governor .... Matthew 2:6
27. Head of the Church .... Ephesians 5:23
28. Heir .... Hebrews 1:2
29. Holy One .... Isaiah 41:14; Mark 1:24
30. I am .... John 8:58

58. Resurrection and Life .... John 11:25
59. Righteous One .... 1 Corinthians 1:30
60. Rock .... Matthew 16:18
61. Saviour, Christ the Lord .... Luke 2:11; Titus 2:13;
                                          2 Timothy 1:10
62. Saviour of the World .... 1 John 4:14
63. The Seed .... Genesis 15:5;
                                          Galatians 3:16
64. Servant .... Isaiah 42:1; 49:7
65. The Servant of the Lord .... Isaiah 42:1; 52:13;
                                          Philippians 2:7
66. Good Shepherd .... John 10:11
67. Shiloh .... Genesis 49:10;
                                          Ezekiel 21:27
68. Son of the Blessed .... Mark 14:61
69. Son of David .... Matthew 12:23
70. Son of God .... John 10:36
71. Son of Man .... Mark 10:45
72. The Son .... Psalm 2:7;
                                          Hebrews 5:8
73. The Son of Man .... Daniel 7:13;
                                          Matthew 20:28
74. Stone .... Matthew 21:42;
                                          1 Peter 2:8
75. The Stone .... Psalm 118:22;
                                          1 Peter 2:4-8
76. Teacher .... John 3:2;
                                          Matthew 9:11
77. Truth .... John 14:6
78. True Vine .... John 15:1
79. The Way .... John 14:6
80. Wonderful .... Isaiah 9:6;
                                          John 1:14
81. Word .... John 1:1

HIS HUMILITY

For he shall grow up before him as a tender plant, and as a root out of a dry ground: he hath no form nor comeliness; and when we shall see him, there is no beauty that we should desire him.

He is despised and rejected of men; a man of sorrows, and acquainted with grief: and we hid as it were our faces from him; he was despised, and we esteemed him not.

Isaiah 53:2, 3

Rejoice greatly, O daughter of Zion; shout, O daughter of Jerusalem: behold, thy King cometh unto thee: he is just, and having salvation; lowly, and riding upon an ass. . . .

Zechariah 9:9

Tell ye the daughter of Sion, Behold, thy King cometh unto thee, meek, and sitting upon an ass, and a colt the foal of an ass.

Matthew 21:5

Take my yoke upon you, and learn of me; for I am meek and lowly in heart: and ye shall find rest unto your souls.

Matthew 11:29

For whether is greater, he that sitteth at meat, or he that serveth? is not he that sitteth at meat? but I am among you as he that serveth.

Luke 22:27

And I seek not mine own glory: there is one that seeketh and judgeth.

John 8:50

Jesus knowing that the Father had given all things into his hands, and that he was come from God, and went to God;

He riseth from supper, and laid aside his garments; and took a towel, and girded himself.

After that he poureth water into a bason, and began to wash the disciples' feet, and to wipe them with the towel wherewith he was girded.

John 13:3-5

Who, being in the form of God, thought it not robbery to be equal with God:

But made himself of no reputation, and took upon him the form of a servant, and was made in the likeness of men:

And being found in fashion as a man, he humbled himself, and became obedient unto death, even the death of the cross.

Philippians 2:6-8

Even as the Son of man came not to be ministered unto, but to minister, and to give his life a ransom for many.

Matthew 20:28

And in thy majesty ride prosperously because of truth and meekness and righteousness; and thy right hand shall teach thee terrible things.

Psalm 45:4

He shall not cry, nor lift up, nor cause his voice to be heard in the street.

Isaiah 42:2

Who did no sin, neither was guile found in his mouth:

Who, when he was reviled, reviled not again; when he suffered, he threatened not; but committed himself to him that judgeth righteously.

1 Peter 2:22, 23

* * * *

The LORD God hath opened mine ear, and I was not rebellious, neither turned away back.

I gave my back to the smiters, and my cheeks to them that plucked off the hair: I hid not my face from shame and spitting.

Isaiah 50:5, 6

For consider him that endured such contradiction of sinners against himself, lest ye be wearied and faint in your minds.

Hebrews 12:3

He was oppressed, and he was afflicted, yet he opened not his mouth: he is brought as a lamb to the slaughter, and as a sheep before her shearers is dumb, so he openeth not his mouth.

Isaiah 53:7

The place of the scripture which he read was this, He was led as a sheep to the slaughter; and like a lamb dumb before his shearer, so opened he not his mouth.

Acts 8:32

110

HIS OFFICE

As Prophet

The LORD thy God will raise up unto thee a Prophet from the midst of thee, of thy brethren, like unto me; unto him ye shall hearken;

According to all that thou desiredst of the LORD thy God in Horeb in the day of the assembly, saying, Let me not hear again the voice of the LORD my God, neither let me see this great fire any more, that I die not.

And the LORD said unto me, They have well spoken that which they have spoken.

I will raise them up a Prophet from among their brethren, like unto thee, and will put my words in his mouth; and he shall speak unto them all that I shall command him.

Deuteronomy 18:15-18

And he shall send Jesus Christ, which before was preached unto you:

Whom the heaven must receive until the times of restitution of all things, which God hath spoken by the mouth of all his holy prophets since the world began.

Acts 3:20, 21

Moses truly said unto the fathers, A prophet shall the LORD your God raise up unto you of your brethren, like unto me; him shall ye hear in all things whatsoever he shall say unto you.

And it shall come to pass, that every soul, which will not hear that prophet, shall be destroyed from among the people.

Yea, and all the prophets from Samuel and those that follow after, as many as have spoken, have likewise foretold of these days.

Ye are the children of the prophets, and of the covenant which God made with our fathers, saying unto Abraham, And in thy seed shall all the kindreds of the earth be blessed.

Unto you first God, having raised up his Son Jesus, sent him to bless you, in turning away every one of you from his iniquities.

Acts 3:22-26

God, who at sundry times and in divers manners spake in time past unto the fathers by the prophets,

Hath in these last days spoken unto us by his Son, whom he hath appointed heir of all things, by whom also he made the worlds.

Hebrews 1:1, 2

And the multitude said, This is Jesus the prophet of Nazareth of Galilee.

Matthew 21:11

Others said, That it is Elias. And others said, That it is a prophet, or as one of the prophets.

Mark 6:15

As Priest

And take thou unto thee Aaron thy brother, and his sons with him, from among the children of Israel, that he may minister unto me in the priest's office, even Aaron, Nadab and Abihu, Eleazar and Ithamar, Aaron's sons.

Exodus 28:1

And no man taketh this honour unto himself, but he that is called of God, as was Aaron.

So also Christ glorified not himself to be made an high priest; but he that said unto him, Thou art my Son, to day have I begotten thee.

Hebrews 5:4, 5

* * * *

To be a memorial unto the children of Israel, that no stranger, which is not of the seed of Aaron, come near to offer incense before the LORD; that he be not as Korah, and as his company: as the LORD said to him by the hand of Moses.

Numbers 16:40

As he saith also in another place, Thou art a priest for ever after the order of Melchisedec.

Called of God an high priest after the order of Melchisedec.

Hebrews 5:6, 10

The LORD hath sworn, and will not repent, Thou art a priest for ever after the order of Melchizedek.

Psalm 110:4

Whither the forerunner is for us entered, even Jesus, made an high priest for ever after the order of Melchisedec.

Hebrews 6:20

Seeing then that we have a great high priest, that is passed into the heavens, Jesus the Son of God, let us hold fast our profession.

Hebrews 4:14

If therefore perfection were by the Levitical priesthood, (for under it the people received the law,) what further need was there that another priest should rise after the order of Melchisedec, and not be called after the order of Aaron?

For the priesthood being changed, there is made of necessity a change also of the law.

For he of whom these things are spoken pertaineth to another tribe, of which no man gave attendance at the altar.

For it is evident that our LORD sprang out of Juda; of which tribe Moses spake nothing concerning priesthood.

And it is yet far more evident: for that after the similtude of Melchisedec there ariseth another priest,

Who is made, not after the law of a carnal commandment, but after the power of an endless life.

For he testifieth, Thou art a priest for ever after the order of Melchisedec.

For there is verily a disannulling of the commandment going before for the weakness and unprofitableness thereof.

For the law made nothing perfect, but the bringing in of a better hope did; by the which we draw nigh unto God.

And inasmuch as not without an oath he was made priest:

(For those priests were made without an oath; but this with an oath by him that said unto him, The LORD sware and will not repent, Thou art a priest for ever after the order of Melchisedec:)

By so much was Jesus made a surety of a better testament.

Hebrews 7:11-22

* * * *

And Melchizedek king of Salem brought forth bread and wine: and he was the priest of the most high God.

Genesis 14:18

For this Melchisedec, king of Salem, priest of the most high God, who met Abraham returning from the slaughter of the kings, and blessed him;

To whom also Abraham gave a tenth part of all; first being by interpretation King of righteousness, and after that also King of Salem, which is, King of peace.

Hebrews 7:1, 2

* * * *

The LORD said unto my LORD, Sit thou at my right hand, until I make thine enemies thy footstool.

Psalm 110:1

Behold, the days come, saith the LORD, that I will perform that good thing which I have promised unto the house of Israel and to the house of Judah.

In those days, and at that time, will I cause the Branch of righteousness to grow up unto David; and he shall execute judgment and righteousness in the land.

In those days shall Judah be saved, and Jerusalem shall dwell safely: and this is the name wherewith she shall be called, The LORD our righteousness.

Jeremiah 33:14-16

But they shall serve the LORD their God, and David their king, whom I will raise up unto them.

And their nobles shall be of themselves, and their governor shall proceed from the midst of them; and I will cause him to draw near, and he shall approach unto me: for who is this that engaged his heart to approach unto me? saith the LORD.

And ye shall be my people, and I will be your God.

Jeremiah 30:9, 21, 22

Behold, the days come, saith the LORD, that I will make a

new covenant with the house of Israel, and with the house of Judah.

Jeremiah 31:31

While the Pharisees were gathered together, Jesus asked them, Saying, What think ye of Christ? whose son is he? They say unto him, The son of David.

He saith unto them, How then doth David in spirit call him LORD, saying,

The LORD said unto my LORD, Sit thou on my right hand, till I make thine enemies thy footstool?

Matthew 22:41-42

But this man, after he had offered one sacrifice for sins for ever, sat down on the right hand of God;

From henceforth expecting till his enemies be made his footstool.

Hebrews 10:12, 13

To open the blind eyes, to bring out the prisoners from the prison, and them that sit in darkness out of the prison house.

Isaiah 42:7

And ye shall know the truth, and the truth shall make you free.

If the Son therefore shall make you free, ye shall be free indeed.

John 8:32, 36

Stand fast therefore in the liberty wherewith Christ hath made us free, and be not entangled again with the yoke of bondage.

Galatians 5:1

* * * *

As Morning Star

I shall see him, but not now: I shall behold him, but not nigh: there shall come a Star out of Jacob, and a Sceptre shall rise out of Israel, and shall smite the corners of Moab, and destroy all the children of Sheth.

Numbers 24:17

115

We have also a more sure word of prophecy; whereunto ye do well that ye take heed, as unto a light that shineth in a dark place, until the day dawn, and the day star arise in your hearts.

2 Peter 1:19

And I will give him the morning star.

Revelation 2:28

I Jesus have sent mine angel to testify unto you these things in the churches. I am the root and the offspring of David, and the bright and morning star.

Revelation 22:16

HIS SACRIFICE and ATONEMENT

But your iniquities have separated between you and your God, and your sins have hid his face from you, that he will not hear.

Isaiah 59:2

For the life of the flesh is in the blood: and I have given it to you upon the altar to make an atonement for your souls: for it is the blood that maketh an atonement for the soul.

Leviticus 17:11

The next day John seeth Jesus coming unto him, and saith, Behold the Lamb of God, which taketh away the sin of the world.

John 1:29

By the which will we are sanctified through the offering of the body of Jesus Christ once for all.

Hebrews 10:10

For this is my blood of the new testament, which is shed for many for the remission of sins.

Matthew 26:28

But God commendeth his love toward us, in that, while we were yet sinners, Christ died for us.

Much more then, being now justified by his blood, we shall be saved from wrath through him.

For if, when we were enemies, we were reconciled to God by the death of his Son, much more, being reconciled, we shall be saved by his life.

Romans 5:8-10

*   *   *   *

And Aaron shall bring the goat upon which the LORD's lot fell, and offer him for a sin offering.

And the goat shall bear upon him all their iniquities unto a land not inhabited: and he shall let go the goat in the wilderness.

And he shall make an atonement for the holy sanctuary, and he shall make an atonement for the tabernacle of the congregation, and for the altar, and he shall make an atonement for the priests, and for all the people of the congregation.

Leviticus 16:9, 22, 33

For then must he often have suffered since the foundation of the world: but now once in the end of the world hath he appeared to put away sin by the sacrifice of himself.

Hebrews 9:26

All we like sheep have gone astray; we have turned every one to his own way; and the Lord hath laid on him the iniquity of us all.

Isaiah 53:6

Forasmuch as ye know that ye were not redeemed with corruptible things, as silver and gold, from your vain conversation received by tradition from your fathers;

But with the precious blood of Christ, as of a lamb without blemish and without spot.

1 Peter 1:18, 19

Who his own self bare our sins in his own body on the tree, that we, being dead to sins, should live unto righteousness: by whose stripes ye were healed.

1 Peter 2:24

*   *   *   *

For he hath made him to be sin for us, who knew no sin; that we might be made the righteousness of God in him.

2 Corinthians 5:21

*   *   *   *

Your lamb shall be without blemish, a male of the first year: ye shall take it out from the sheep, or from the goats:

And ye shall keep it up until the fourteenth day of the same month: and the whole assembly of the congregation of Israel shall kill it in the evening.

And they shall take of the blood, and strike it on the two side posts and on the upper door post of the houses, wherein they shall eat it.

That ye shall say, It is the sacrifice of the LORD'S passover, who passed over the houses of the children of Israel in Egypt, when he smote the Egyptians, and delivered our houses. And the people bowed the head and worshipped.

Exodus 12:5-7, 27

Purge out therefore the old leaven, that ye may be a new lump, as ye are unleavened. For even Christ our passover is sacrificed for us.

1 Corinthians 5:7

*   *   *   *

Yet it pleased the LORD to bruise him; he hath put him to grief: when thou shalt make his soul an offering for sin, he shall see his seed, he shall prolong his days, and the pleasure of the LORD shall prosper in his hand.

He shall see of the travail of his soul, and shall be satisfied: by his knowledge shall my righteous servant justify many; for he shall bear their iniquities.

Isaiah 53:10, 11

And thou shalt take the atonement money of the children of Israel, and shalt appoint it for the service of the tabernacle of the congregation; that it may be a memorial unto the children of Israel before the LORD, to make an atonement for your souls.

Exodus 30:16

And he took bread, and gave thanks, and brake it, and gave unto them, saying, This is my body which is given for you: this do in remembrance of me.

Likewise also the cup after supper, saying, This cup is the new testament in my blood, which is shed for you.

Luke 22:19, 20

And every priest standeth daily ministering and offering oftentimes the same sacrifices, which can never take away sins:

But this man, after he had offered one sacrifice for sins for ever, sat down on the right hand of God;

From henceforth expecting till his enemies be made his footstool.

For by one offering he hath perfected for ever them that are sanctified.

Whereof the Holy Ghost also is a witness to us: for after that he had said before,

This is the covenant that I will make with them after those days, saith the LORD, I will put my laws into their hearts, and in their minds will I write them;

And their sins and iniquities will I remember no more.

Hebrews 10:11-17

But if we walk in the light, as he is in the light, we have fellowship one with another, and the blood of Jesus Christ his Son cleanseth us from all sin.

1 John 1:7

And from Jesus Christ, who is the faithful witness, and the first begotten of the dead, and the prince of the kings of the earth. Unto him that loved us, and washed us from our sins in his own blood.

Revelation 1:5

Sacrifice and offering thou didst not desire; mine ears hast thou opened: burnt offering and sin offering hast thou not required.

I delight to do thy will, O my God: yea, thy law is within my heart.

Psalm 40:6, 8

*   *   *   *

Wherefore when he cometh into the world, he saith, Sacrifice and offering thou wouldest not, but a body hast thou prepared me:

In burnt offerings and sacrifices for sin thou hast had no pleasure.

Then said I, Lo, I come (in the volume of the book it is written of me,) to do thy will, O God.

Hebrews 10:5-7

*   *   *   *

120

Deliver me from bloodguiltiness, O God, thou God of my salvation: and my tongue shall sing aloud of thy righteousness.

For thou desirest not sacrifice; else would I give it: thou delightest not in burnt offering.

The sacrifices of God are a broken spirit: a broken and a contrite heart, O God, thou wilt not despise.

Psalms 51:14, 16, 17

For I desired mercy, and not sacrifice; and the knowledge of God more than burnt offerings.

Hosea 6:6

To what purpose is the multitude of your sacrifices unto me? saith the LORD: I am full of the burnt offerings of rams, and the fat of fed beasts; and I delight not in the blood of bullocks, or of lambs, or of he goats.

Isaiah 1:11

But when Jesus heard that, he said unto them, They that be whole need not a physician, but they that are sick.

But go ye and learn what that meaneth, I will have mercy, and not sacrifice: for I am not come to call the righteous, but sinners to repentance.

Matthew 9:12, 13

Which was a figure for the time then present, in which were offered both gifts and sacrifices, that could not make him that did the service perfect, as pertaining to the conscience.

Hebrews 9:9

HIS THRONE

Of the increase of his government and peace there shall be no end, upon the throne of David, and upon his kingdom, to order it, and to establish it with judgment and with justice from henceforth even for ever. The zeal of the LORD of hosts will perform this.

Isaiah 9:7

Behold, a king shall reign in righteousness, and princes shall rule in judgment.

Isaiah 32:1

Yet have I set my king upon my holy hill of Zion.

Psalm 2:6

And the angel said unto her, Fear not, Mary: for thou hast found favour with God.

And, behold, thou shalt conceive in thy womb, and bring forth a son, and shalt call his name JESUS.

He shall be great, and shall be called the Son of the Highest: and the LORD God shall give unto him the throne of his father David:

And he shall reign over the house of Jacob for ever; and of his kingdom there shall be no end.

Luke 1:30-33

For unto us a child is born, unto us a son is given: and the government shall be upon his shoulder: and his name shall be called Wonderful, Counsellor, The mighty God, The everlasting Father, The Prince of Peace.

Isaiah 9:6

For unto you is born this day in the city of David a Saviour, which is Christ the LORD.

Luke 2:11

*   *   *   *

I shall see him, but not now: I shall behold him, but not nigh: there shall come a Star out of Jacob, and a Sceptre shall rise out of Israel, and shall smite the corners of Moab, and destroy all the children of Sheth.

Numbers 24:17

And out of his mouth goeth a sharp sword, that with it he should smite the nations: and he shall rule them with a rod of iron: and he treadeth the winepress of the fierceness and wrath of Almighty God.

Revelation 19:15

* * * *

Thy throne, O God, is for ever and ever: the sceptre of thy kingdom is a right sceptre.

Psalm 45:6

But unto the Son he saith, Thy throne, O God, is for ever and ever: a sceptre of righteousness is the sceptre of thy kingdom.

Hebrews 1:8

* * * *

In the year that king Uzziah died I saw also the LORD sitting upon a throne, high and lifted up, and his train filled the temple.

Isaiah 6:1

These things said Esaias, when he saw his glory, and spake of him.

John 12:41

* * * *

And the key of the house of David will I lay upon his shoulder; so he shall open, and none shall shut; and he shall shut, and none shall open.

Isaiah 22:22

And unto the angel of the church of the Laodiceans write; These things saith the Amen, the faithful and true witness, the beginning of the creation of God;

I know thy works, that thou art neither cold nor hot: I would thou wert cold or hot.

So then because thou art lukewarm, and neither cold nor hot, I will spue thee out of my mouth.

Because thou sayest, I am rich, and increased with goods, and have need of nothing; and knowest not that thou are wretched, and miserable, and poor, and blind, and naked:

I counsel thee to buy of me gold tried in the fire, that thou mayest be rich; and white raiment, that thou mayest be clothed, and that the shame of thy nakedness do not appear; and anoint thine eyes with eyesalve, that thou mayest see.

As many as I love, I rebuke and chasten: be zealous therefore, and repent.

Behold, I stand at the door, and knock: if any man hear my voice, and open the door, I will come in to him, and will sup with him, and he with me.

To him that overcometh will I grant to sit with me in my throne, even as I also overcame, and am set down with my Father in his throne.

Revelation 3:14-21

After this I beheld, and, lo, a great multitude, which no man could number, of all nations, and kindreds, and people, and tongues, stood before the throne, and before the Lamb, clothed in white robes, and palms in their hands;

And cried with a loud voice, saying, Salvation to our God which sitteth upon the throne, and unto the Lamb.

And one of the elders answered, saying unto me, What are these which are arrayed in white robes? and whence came they?

And I said unto him, Sir, thou knowest. And he said to me, These are they which came out of great tribulation, and have washed their robes, and made them white in the blood of the Lamb.

Revelation 7:9, 10, 13, 14

Therefore are they before the throne of God, and serve him day and night in his temple: and he that sitteth on the throne shall dwell among them.

They shall hunger no more, neither thirst any more; neither shall the sun light on them, nor any heat.

For the Lamb which is in the midst of the throne shall feed them, and shall lead them unto living fountains of waters: and God shall wipe away all tears from their eyes.

Revelation 7:15-17

And I saw thrones, and they sat upon them, and judgment was given unto them: and I saw the souls of them that were beheaded for the witness of Jesus, and for the word of God, and which had not worshipped the beast, neither his image, neither had received his mark upon their foreheads, or in their hands; and they lived and reigned with Christ a thousand years.

But the rest of the dead lived not again until the thousand years were finished. This is the first resurrection.

Blessed and holy is he that hath part in the first resurrection: on such the second death hath no power, but they shall be priests of God and of Christ, and shall reign with him a thousand years.

Revelation 20:4-6

HIS ULTIMATE VICTORY
OVER SIN

And I will put enmity between thee and the woman, and between thy seed and her seed; it shall bruise thy head, and thou shalt bruise his heel.

Genesis 3:15

Forasmuch then as the children are partakers of flesh and blood, he also himself likewise took part of the same; that through death he might destroy him that had the power of death, that is, the devil.

Hebrews 2:14

And they overcame him by the blood of the Lamb, and by the word of their testimony; and they loved not their lives unto the death.

Revelation 12:11

Blotting out the handwriting of ordinances that was against us, which was contrary to us, and took it out of the way, nailing it to his cross;

And having spoiled principalities and powers, he made a shew of them openly, triumphing over them in it.

Colossians 2:14, 15

O death, where is thy sting? O grave, where is thy victory?

The sting of death is sin; and the strength of sin is the law.

But thanks be to God, which giveth us the victory through our LORD Jesus Christ.

1 Corinthians 15:55-57

And the devil that deceived them was cast into the lake of fire and brimstone, where the beast and the false prophet are, and shall be tormented day and night for ever and ever.

Revelation 20:10

*　*　*　*

The LORD said unto my LORD, Sit thou at my right hand, until I make thine enemies thy footstool.

Psalm 110:1

Who being the brightness of his glory, and the express image of his person, and upholding all things by the word of his power, when he had by himself purged our sins, sat down on the right hand of the Majesty on high.

Hebrews 1:3

So then after the LORD had spoken unto them, he was received up into heaven, and sat on the right hand of God.

Mark 16:19

For David is not ascended into the heavens: but he saith himself, The LORD said unto my LORD, Sit thou on my right hand,

Until I make thy foes thy footstool.

Acts 2:34, 35

HIS RETURN

Our God shall come, and shall not keep silence: a fire shall devour before him, and it shall be very tempestuous round about him.

He shall call to the heavens from above, and to the earth, that he may judge his people.

Gather my saints together unto me; those that have made a covenant with me by sacrifice.

Gather my saints together unto me; those that have made a covenant with me by sacrifice.

And the heavens shall declare his righteousness: for God is judge himself. Selah.

Psalm 50:3-6

And as it is appointed unto men once to die, but after this the judgment:

So Christ was once offered to bear the sins of many; and unto them that look for him shall he appear the second time without sin unto salvation.

Hebrews 9:27, 28

* * * *

I saw in the night visions, and, behold, one like the Son of man came with the clouds of heaven, and came to the Ancient of days, and they brought him near before him.

And there was given him dominion, and glory, and a kingdom, that all people, nations, and languages, should serve him: his dominion is an everlasting dominion, which shall not pass away, and his kingdom that which shall not be destroyed.

Daniel 7:13, 14

And then shall appear the sign of the Son of man in heaven: and then shall all the tribes of the earth mourn, and they shall see the Son of man coming in the clouds of heaven with power and great glory.

Matthew 24:30

Jesus saith unto him, Thou hast said: nevertheless I say unto you, Hereafter shall ye see the Son of man sitting on the right hand of power, and coming in the clouds of heaven.

Matthew 26:64

And then shall they see the Son of man coming in the clouds with great power and glory.

And Jesus said, I am: and ye shall see the Son of man sitting on the right hand of power, and coming in the clouds of heaven.

Mark 13:26; 14:62

And in the midst of the seven candlesticks one like unto the Son of man, clothed with a garment down to the foot, and girt about the paps with a golden girdle.

Revelation 1:13

And I looked, and behold a white cloud, and upon the cloud one sat like unto the Son of man, having on his head a golden crown, and in his hand a sharp sickle.

Revelation 14:14

*   *   *   *

And I will pour upon the house of David, and upon the inhabitants of Jerusalem, the spirit of grace and of supplications: and they shall look upon me whom they have pierced, and they shall mourn for him, as one mourneth for his only son, and shall be in bitterness for him, as one that is in bitterness for his firstborn.

In that day shall there be a great mourning in Jerusalem, as the mourning of Hadadrimmon in the valley of Megiddon.

Zechariah 12:10, 11

Behold, he cometh with clouds; and every eye shall see him, and they also which pierced him: and all kindreds of the earth shall wail because of him. Even so, Amen.

Revelation 1:7

And again another scripture saith, They shall look on him whom they pierced.

John 19:37

And then shall appear the sign of the Son of man in heaven: and then shall all the tribes of the earth mourn, and

129

they shall see the Son of man coming in the clouds of heaven with power and great glory.

Matthew 24:30

* * * *

And his feet shall stand in that day upon the mount of Olives, which is before Jerusalem on the east, and the mount of Olives shall cleave in the midst thereof toward the east and toward the west, and there shall be a very great valley; and half of the mountain shall remove toward the north, and half of it toward the south.

And ye shall flee to the valley of the mountains; for the valley of the mountains shall reach unto Azal: yea, ye shall flee, like as ye fled from before the earthquake in the days of Uzziah king of Judah: and the LORD my God shall come, and all the saints with thee.

And it shall come to pass in that day, that the light shall not be clear, nor dark:

But it shall be one day which shall be known to the LORD, not day, nor night: but it shall come to pass, that at evening time it shall be light.

And it shall be in that day, that living waters shall go out from Jerusalem; half of them toward the former sea, and half of them toward the hinder sea: in summer and in winter shall it be.

Zechariah 14:4-8

For they are the spirits of devils, working miracles, which go forth unto the kings of the earth and of the whole world, to gather them to the battle of that great day of God Almighty.

Revelation 16:14

For the Son of man shall come in the glory of his Father with his angels; and then he shall reward every man according to his works.

Matthew 16:27

And I will shew wonders in heaven above, and signs in the earth beneath; blood, and fire, and vapour of smoke:

130

The sun shall be turned into darkness, and the moon into blood, before that great and notable day of the LORD come.

Acts 2:19, 20

And he shewed me a pure river of water of life, clear as crystal, proceeding out of the throne of God and of the Lamb.

In the midst of the street of it, and on either side of the river, was there the tree of life, which bare twelve manner of fruits, and yielded her fruit every month: and the leaves of the tree were for the healing of the nations.

Revelation 22:1, 2

Before she travailed, she brought forth; before her pain came, she was delivered of a man child.

Who hath heard such a thing? who hath seen such things? Shall the earth be made to bring forth in one day? or shall a nation be born at once? for as soon as Zion travailed, she brought forth her children.

Shall I bring to the birth, and not cause to bring forth? saith the LORD: shall I cause to bring forth, and shut the womb? saith thy God.

Isaiah 66:7-9

And so all Israel shall be saved: as it is writtten, There shall come out of Sion the Deliverer, and shall turn away ungodliness from Jacob.

Romans 11:26

*　*　*　*

For, behold, the LORD will come with fire, and with his chariots like a whirlwind, to render his anger with fury, and his rebuke with flames of fire.

For by fire and by his sword will the LORD plead with all flesh: and the slain of the LORD shall be many.

Isaiah 66:15, 16

Seeing it is a righteous thing with God to recompense tribulation to them that trouble you;

And to you who are troubled rest with us, when the LORD Jesus shall be revealed from heaven with his mighty angels,

In flaming fire taking vengeance on them that know not God, and that obey not the gospel of our LORD Jesus Christ:

Who shall be punished with everlasting destruction from the presence of the LORD, and from the glory of his power.

2 Thessalonians 1:6-9

* * * *

For I know that my redeemer liveth, and that he shall stand at the latter day upon the earth:

And though after my skin worms destroy this body, yet in my flesh shall I see God:

Whom I shall see for myself, and mine eyes shall behold, and not another; though my reins be consumed within me.

Job 19:25-27

For he hath put all things under his feet. But when he saith all things are put under him, it is manifest that he is excepted, which did put all things under him.

And when all things shall be subdued unto him, then shall the Son also himself be subject unto him that put all things under him, that God may be all in all.

In a moment, in the twinkling of an eye, at the last trump: for the trumpet shall sound, and the dead shall be raised incorruptible, and we shall be changed.

1 Corinthians 15:27, 28, 52

For the LORD himself shall descend from heaven with a shout, with the voice of the archangel, and with the trump of God: and the dead in Christ shall rise first.

1 Thessalonians 4:16

For yourselves know perfectly that the day of the LORD so cometh as a thief in the night.

For when they shall say, Peace and safety; then sudden destruction cometh upon them, as travail upon a woman with child; and they shall not escape.

1 Thessalonians 5:2, 3

* * * *

Yet have I set my king upon my holy hill of Zion.

I will declare the decree: the LORD hath said unto me, Thou art my Son; this day have I begotten thee.

Ask of me, and I shall give thee the heathen for thine inheritance, and the uttermost parts of the earth for thy possession.

Thou shalt break them with a rod of iron; thou shalt dash them in pieces like a potter's vessel.

Psalm 2:6-9

And she brought forth a man child, who was to rule all nations with a rod of iron: and her child was caught up unto God, and to his throne.

Revelation 12:5

And out of his mouth goeth a sharp sword, that with it he should smite the nations: and he shall rule them with a rod of iron: and he treadeth the winepress of the fierceness and wrath of Almighty God.

Revelation 19:15

When the Son of man shall come in his glory, and all the holy angels with him, then shall he sit upon the throne of his glory.

Matthew 25:31

When he shall come to be glorified in his saints, and to be admired in all them that believe (because our testimony among you was believed) in that day.

2 Thessalonians 1:10

* * * *

Before the LORD: for he cometh, for he cometh to judge the earth: he shall judge the world with righteousness, and the people with his truth.

Psalm 96:13

And I saw heaven opened, and behold a white horse; and he that sat upon him was called Faithful and True, and in righteousness he doth judge and make war.

Revelation 19:11

133

HIS PRE-EXISTENCE

And God said, Let us make man in our image, after our likeness: and let them have dominion over the fish of the sea, and over the fowl of the air, and over the cattle, and over all the earth, and over every creeping thing that creepeth upon the earth.

Genesis 1:26

In the beginning was the Word, and the Word was with God, and the Word was God.

All things were made by him; and without him was not any thing made that was made.

John 1:1, 3

Your father Abraham rejoiced to see my day: and he saw it, and was glad.

Then said the Jews unto him, Thou art not yet fifty years old, and hast thou seen Abraham?

Jesus said unto them, Verily, verily, I say unto you, Before Abraham was, I am.

John 8:56-58

* * * *

But thou art the same, and thy years shall have no end.

Psalm 102:27

Jesus Christ the same yesterday, and to day, and for ever.

Hebrews 13:8

I am Alpha and Omega, the beginning and the end, the first and the last.

Revelation 22:13

* * * *

For I am the LORD, I change not; therefore ye sons of Jacob are not consumed.

Malachi 3:6

And now, O Father, glorify thou me with thine own self with the glory which I had with thee before the world was.

John 17:5

134

Father, I will that they also, whom thou hast given me, be with me where I am; that they may behold my glory, which thou hast given me: for thou lovedst me before the foundation of the world.

John 17:24

* * * *

Of old hast thou laid the foundation of the earth: and the heavens are the work of thy hands.

They shall perish, but thou shalt endure: yea, all of them shall wax old like a garment; as a vesture shalt thou change them, and they shall be changed.

Psalm 102:25, 26

But unto the Son he saith, Thy throne, O God, is for ever and ever: a sceptre of righteousness is the sceptre of thy kingdom.

Thou hast loved righteousness, and hated iniquity; therefore God, even thy God, hath anointed thee with the oil of gladness above thy fellows.

And, Thou, LORD, in the beginning hast laid the foundation of the earth; and the heavens are the works of thine hands:

They shall perish; but thou remainest; and they all shall wax old as doth a garment;

And as a vesture shalt thou fold them up, and they shall be changed: but thou art the same, and thy years shall not fail.

Hebrews 1:8-12

* * * *

The LORD possessed me in the beginning of his way, before his works of old.

I was set up from everlasting, from the beginning, or ever the earth was.

When there were no depths, I was brought forth; when there were no fountains abounding with water.

Before the mountains were settled, before the hills was I brought forth:

While as yet he had not made the earth, nor the fields, nor the highest part of the dust of the world.

135

When he prepared the heavens, I was there: when he set a compass upon the face of the depth:

When he established the clouds above: when he strengthened the fountains of the deep:

When he gave to the sea his decree, that the waters should not pass his commandment: when he appointed the foundations of the earth:

Then I was by him, as one brought up with him: and I was daily his delight, rejoicing always before him;

Rejoicing in the habitable part of his earth; and my delights were with the sons of men.

Now therefore hearken unto me, O ye children: for blessed are they that keep my ways.

Proverbs 8:22-32

Who being the brightness of his glory, and the express image of his person, and upholding all things by the word of his power, when he had by himself purged our sins, sat down on the right hand of the Majesty on high.

Hebrews 1:3

Who is the image of the invisible God, the firstborn of every creature:

THE SON OF GOD

I will declare the decree: The LORD hath said unto me, Thou art my Son; this day have I begotten thee.

Psalm 2:7

And it shall come to pass, when thy days be expired that thou must go to be with thy fathers, that I will raise up thy seed after thee, which shall be of thy sons; and I will establish his kingdom.

He shall build me an house, and I will stablish his throne for ever.

I will be his father, and he shall be my son: and I will not take my mercy away from him, as I took it from him that was before thee:

But I will settle him in mine house and in my kingdom for ever: and his throne shall be established for evermore.

1 Chronicles 17:11-14

And when thy days be fulfilled, and thou shalt sleep with thy fathers, I will set up thy seed after thee, which shall proceed out of thy bowels, and I will establish his kingdom.

He shall build an house for my name, and I will stablish the throne of his kingdom for ever.

I will be his father, and he shall be my son. If he commit iniquity, I will chasten him with the rod of men, and with the stripes of the children of men:

But my mercy shall not depart away from him, as I took if from Saul, whom I put away before thee.

And thine house and thy kingdom shall be established for ever before thee: thy throne shall be established for ever.

2 Samuel 7:12-16

And Simon Peter answered and said, Thou art the Christ, the Son of the living God.

Matthew 16:16

And lo a voice from heaven, saying, This is my beloved Son, in whom I am well pleased.

Matthew 3:17

And there came a voice out of the cloud, saying, This is my beloved Son: hear him.

Then said they all, Art thou then the Son of God? And he said unto them, Ye say that I am.

But God raised him from the dead:

And he was seen many days of them which came up with him from Galilee to Jerusalem, who are his witnesses unto the people.

And we declare unto you glad tidings, how that the promise which was made unto the fathers,

God hath fulfilled the same unto us their children, in that he hath raised up Jesus again; as it is also written in the second psalm, Thou art my Son, this day have I begotten thee.

Acts 13:30-33

And I saw, and bare record that this is the Son of God.

He saith unto them, Come and see. They came and saw where he dwelt, and abode with him that day: for it was about the tenth hour.

John 1:34, 39

Jesus heard that they had cast him out; and when he had found him, he said unto him, Dost thou believe on the Son of God?

He answered and said, Who is he, LORD, that I might believe on him?

And Jesus said unto him, Thou hast both seen him, and it is he that talketh with thee.

John 9:35-37

* * * *

He shall cry unto me, Thou art my father, my God, and the rock of my salvation.

Also I will make him my firstborn, higher than the kings of the earth.

Psalm 89:26, 27

But last of all he sent unto them his son, saying, They will reverence my son.

Matthew 21:37

But he held his peace, and answered nothing. Again the

138

high priest asked him, and said unto him, Art thou the Christ, the Son of the Blessed?

And Jesus said, I am: and ye shall see the Son of man sitting on the right hand of power, and coming in the clouds of heaven.

Mark 14:61, 62

He shall be great, and shall be called the Son of the Highest: and the LORD God shall give unto him the throne of his father David.

And the angel answered and said unto her, The Holy Ghost shall come upon thee, and the power of the Highest shall overshadow thee: therefore also that holy thing which shall be born of thee shall be called the Son of God.

Luke 1:32, 35

No man hath seen God at any time; the only begotten Son, which is in the bosom of the Father, he hath declared him.

John 1:18

For God so loved the world, that he gave his only begotten Son, that whosoever believeth in him should not perish, but have everlasting life.

For God sent not his Son into the world to condemn the world; but that the world through him might be saved.

He that believeth on him is not condemned: but he that believeth not is comdemned already, because he hath not believed in the name of the only begotten Son of God.

John 3:16-18

Then answered Jesus and said unto them, Verily, verily, I say unto you, The Son can do nothing of himself, but what he seeth the Father do: for what things soever he doeth, these also doeth the Son likewise.

For the Father loveth the Son, and sheweth him all things that himself doeth: and he will shew him greater works than these, that ye may marvel.

For as the Father raiseth up the dead, and quickeneth them; even so the Son quickeneth whom he will.

For the Father judgeth no man, but hath commited all judgment unto the Son:

That all men should honour the Son, even as they honour the Father. He that honoureth not the Son honoureth not the Father which hath sent him.

Verily, verily, I say unto you, He that heareth my word, and believeth on him that sent me, hath everlasting life, and shall not come into condemnation; but is passed from death unto life.

Verily, verily, I say unto you, The hour is coming, and now is, when the dead shall hear the voice of the Son of God: and they that hear shall live.

For as the Father hath life in himself; so hath he given to the Son to have life in himself;

And hath given him authority to execute judgment also, because he is the Son of man.

John 5:19-27

Jesus knowing that the Father had given all things into his hands, and that he was come from God, and went to God.

John 13:3

In the beginning was the Word, and the Word was with God, and the Word was God.

And the Word was made flesh, and dwelt among us, (and we beheld his glory, the glory as of the only begotten of the Father,) full of grace and truth.

John 1:1, 14

HIS MISSION

Behold my servant, whom I uphold; mine elect, in whom my soul delighteth; I have put my spirit upon him: he shall bring forth judgment to the Gentiles.

I the LORD have called thee in righteousness, and will hold thine hand, and will keep thee, and give thee for a covenant of the people, for a light of the Gentiles;

To open the blind eyes, to bring out the prisoners from the prison, and them that sit in darkness out of the prison house.

Isaiah 42:1, 6, 7

And Jesus went about all Galilee, teaching in their synagogues, and preaching the gospel of the kingdom, and healing all manner of sickness and all manner of disease among the people.

Matthew 4:23

A light to lighten the Gentiles, and the glory of thy people Israel.

Luke 2:32

For so hath the LORD commanded us, saying, I have set thee to be a light of the Gentiles, that thou shouldest be for salvation unto the ends of the earth.

Acts 13:47

And in that day there shall be a root of Jesse, which shall stand for an ensign of the people; to it shall the Gentiles seek: and his rest shall be glorious.

Isaiah 11:10

And that the Gentiles might glorify God for his mercy; as it is written, For this cause I will confess to thee among the Gentiles, and sing unto thy name.

And again, Praise the LORD, all ye Gentiles; and laud him, all ye people.

And again, Esaias saith, There shall be a root of Jesse, and he that shall rise to reign over the Gentiles; in him shall the Gentiles trust.

Romans 15:9, 11, 12

* * * *

He is despised and rejected of men; a man of sorrows, and acquainted with grief: and we hid as it were our faces from him; he was despised, and we esteemed him not.

Isaiah 53:3

For in that he himself hath suffered being tempted, he is able to succour them that are tempted.

For we have not an high priest which cannot be touched with the feeling of our infirmities; but was in all points tempted like as we are, yet without sin.

Hebrews 2:18; 4:15

Nevertheless the dimness shall not be such as was in her vexation, when at the first he lightly afflicted the land of Zebulun and the land of Naphtali, and afterward did more grievously afflict her by the way of the sea, beyond Jordan, in Galilee of the nations.

The people that walked in darkness have seen a great light: they that dwell in the land of the shadow of death, upon them hath the light shined.

Isaiah 9:1, 2

And leaving Nazareth, he came and dwelt in Capernaum, which is upon the sea coast, in the borders of Zabulon and Nephthalim:

That it might be fulfilled which was spoken by Esaias the prophet, saying,

The land of Zabulon, and the land of Nephthalim, by the way of the sea, beyond Jordan, Galilee of the Gentiles;

The people which sat in darkness saw great light; and to them which sat in the region and shadow of death light is sprung up.

Matthew 4:13-16

* * * *

For the son dishonoureth the father, the daughter riseth up against her mother, the daughter in law against her mother in law; a man's enemies are the men of his own house.

Micah 7:6

Think not that I am come to send peace on earth: I came not to send peace, but a sword.

For I am come to set a man at variance against his father, and the daughter against her mother, and the daughter in law against her mother in law.

And a man's foes shall be they of his own household.

Matthew 10:34-36

* * * *

Behold my servant, whom I uphold; mine elect, in whom my soul delighteth; I have put my spirit upon him: he shall bring forth judgment to the Gentiles.

He shall not cry, nor lift up, nor cause his voice to be heard in the street.

A bruised reed shall he not break, and the smoking flax shall he not quench: he shall bring forth judgment unto truth.

He shall not fail nor be discouraged, till he have set judgment in the earth: and the isles shall wait for his law.

Isaiah 42:1-4

But when Jesus knew it, he withdrew himself from thence: and great multitudes followed him, and he healed them all;

And charged them that they should not make him know:

That it might be fulfilled which was spoken by Esaias the prophet, saying,

Behold my servant, whom I have chosen; my beloved, in whom my soul is well pleased: I will put my spirit upon him, and he shall shew judgment to the Gentiles.

He shall not strive, nor cry; neither shall any man hear his voice in the streets.

A bruised reed shall he not break, and smoking flax shall he not quench, till he send forth judgment unto victory.

And in his name shall the Gentiles trust.

Matthew 12:15-21

* * * *

For Zion's sake will I not hold my peace, and for Jerusalem's sake I will not rest, until the righteousness thereof go forth as brightness, and the salvation thereof as a lamp that burneth.

And the Gentiles shall see thy righteousness, and all kings thy glory: and thou shalt be called by a new name, which the mouth of the LORD shall name.

Thou shalt also be a crown of glory in the hand of the LORD, and a royal diadem in the hand of thy God.

Isaiah 62:1-3

The Spirit of the LORD is upon me, because he hath anointed me to preach the gospel to the poor; he hath sent me to heal the brokenhearted, to preach deliverance to the captives, and recovering of sight to the blind, to set at liberty them that are bruised,

To preach the acceptable year of the LORD.

Luke 4:18, 19

*　*　*　*

But who may abide the day of his coming? and who shall stand when he appeareth? for he is like a refiner's fire, and like fullers' sope:

And he shall sit as a refiner and purifier of silver: and he shall purify the sons of Levi, and purge them as gold and silver, that they may offer unto the LORD an offering in righteousness.

Malachi 3:2, 3

I indeed baptize you with water unto repentance: but he that cometh after me is mightier than I, whose shoes I am not worthy to bear: he shall baptize you with the Holy Ghost, and with fire.

Matthew 3:11, 12

HIS RELATIONSHIP
WITH THE FATHER

The LORD said unto my LORD, Sit thou at my right hand, until I make thine enemies thy footstool.

Psalm 110:1

He saith unto them, How then doth David in spirit call him LORD, saying.

Matthew 22:43

In the beginning was the Word, and the Word was with God, and the Word was God.

John 1:1

* * * *

Hear, O Israel: the LORD our God is one LORD.

Deuteronomy 6:4

But to us there is but one God, the Father, of whom are all things, and we in him; and one LORD Jesus Christ, by whom are all things, and we by him.

1 Corinthians 8:6

But Jesus answered them, My Father worketh hitherto, and I work.

Therefore the Jews sought the more to kill him, because he not only had broken the sabbath, but said also that God was his Father, making himself equal with God.

John 5:17, 18

I and my Father are one.

John 10:30

Jesus cried and said, He that believeth on me, believeth not on me, but on him that sent me.

And he that seeth me seeth him that sent me.

John 12:44, 45

Who, being in the form of God, thought it not robbery to be equal with God.

Philippians 2:6

And without controversy great is the mystery of godliness: God was manifest in the flesh, justified in the Spirit, seen of angels, preached unto the Gentiles, believed on in the world, received up into glory.

1 Timothy 3:16

Looking for that blessed hope, and the glorious appearing of the great God and our Saviour Jesus Christ.

Titus 2:13

*   *   *   *

Blessed is the man that trusteth in the LORD, and whose hope the LORD is.

Jeremiah 17:7

Let not your heart be troubled: ye believe in God, believe also in me.

John 14:1

HIS MIRACLES

Then the eyes of the blind shall be opened, and the ears of the deaf shall be unstopped.

Then shall the lame man leap as an hart, and the tongue of the dumb sing: for in the wilderness shall waters break out, and streams in the desert.

Isaiah 35:5, 6

Jesus answered and said unto them, Go and shew John again those things which ye do hear and see:

The blind receive their sight, and the lame walk, the lepers are cleansed, and deaf hear, the dead are raised up, and the poor have the gospel preached to them.

Matthew 11:4, 5

And Jesus went about all the cities and villages, teaching in their synagogues, and preaching the gospel of the kingdom, and healing every sickness and every disease among the people.

Matthew 9:35

* * * *

And the eyes of them that see shall not be dim, and the ears of them that hear shall hearken.

The heart also of the rash shall under whole, and took up his bed, and walked: and on the same day was the sabbath.

John 5:5-9

When he had thus spoken, he spat on the ground, and made clay of the spittle, and he anointed the eyes of the blind man with the clay,

And said unto him, Go, wash in the pool of Siloam, (which is by interpretation, Sent.) He went his way therefore, and washed, and came seeing.

The neighbours therefore, and they which before had seen him that he was blind, said, Is not this he that sat and begged?

Some said, This is he: others said, He is like him: but he said, I am he.

Therefore said they unto him, How were thine eyes opened?

He answered and said, A man that is called Jesus made clay, and anointed mine eyes, and said unto me, Go to the pool of Siloam, and wash: and I went and washed, and I received sight.

John 9:6-11

* * * *

To open the blind eyes, to bring out the prisoners from the prison, and them that sit in darkness out of the prison house.

Isaiah 42:7

Surely he hath borne our griefs, and carried our sorrows: yet we did esteem him stricken, smitten of God, and afflicted.

Isaiah 53:4

But when Jesus knew it, he withdrew himself from thence: and great multitudes followed him, and he healed them all;

And charged them that they should not make him known:

That it might be fulfilled which was spoken by Esaias the prophet, saying,

Behold my servant, whom I have chosen; my beloved, in whom my soul is well pleased: I will put my spirit upon him, and he shall shew judgment to the Gentiles.

He shall not strive, nor cry; neither shall any man hear his voice in the streets.

A bruised reed shall he not break, and smoking flax shall he not quench, till he send forth judgment unto victory.

And in his name shall the Gentiles trust.

Matthew 12:15-21

* * * *

SPECIFIC MIRACLES OF JESUS

RECORDED ONLY IN MATTHEW
RECORDED ONLY IN MARK

RECORDED ONLY IN LUKE

Huge catch of fishes . . . . Luke 5:1-11
Widow's son raised from the dead at Nain . . . . Luke 7:11-17
A crippled woman's infirmity cured . . . . Luke 13:10-17
Healing of a man with dropsy . . . . Luke 14:1-6
Ten lepers cleansed . . . . Luke 17:11-19
Malchus' ear healed . . . . Luke 22:50-51

RECORDED ONLY IN JOHN

Water turned into wine at Cana . . . . John 2:1-11
Nobleman's son cured of fever . . . . John 4:46-54
A lame man cured at the pool of Bethesda . . . . John 5:1-9
Lazarus raised from the dead . . . . John 11:38-44
Catch of 153 fish . . . . John 21:1-14

REPORTED BY MATTHEW AND MARK

Syro-phoenicians's daughter cured . . . . Matthew 15:28;
                                                          Mark 7:24
Four thousand fed . . . . Matthew 15:32;
                                                          Mark 8:1
Fig-tree cursed . . . . Matthew 21:19;
                                                          Mark 11:13-14

REPORTED BY MATTHEW AND LUKE

Demoniac in synagogue cured . . . . Mark 1:23;
                                                          Luke 4:33

REPORTED BY MATTHEW, MARK, LUKE

Leper cured . . . . Matthew 8:2
                                                          Mark 1:40
                                                          Luke 5:12
Peter's mother-in-law cured . . . . Matthew 8:14
                                                          Mark 1:30
                                                          Luke 4:33
Tempest stilled on Sea of Galilee . . . . Matthew 8:23
                                                          Mark 4:37
                                                          Luke 8:22
Demoniacs cured . . . . Matthew 8:28
                                                          Mark 5:1
                                                          Luke 8:26
Paralytic cured . . . . Matthew 9:2
                                                          Mark 2:3
                                                          Luke 5:18
Jairus' daughter raised from the dead . . . . Matthew 9:23
                                                          Mark 5:23
                                                          Luke 8:41
Woman's issue of blood cured . . . . Matthew 9:20
                                                          Mark 5:25
                                                          Luke 8:43

149

Man's withered hand cured .... Matthew 12:10
Mark 3:1
Luke 6:6
Devil cast out of boy .... Matthew 17:14
Mark 9:17
Luke 9:37
Blind man cured .... Matthew 20:30
Mark 10:46
Luke 18:35

REPORTED BY MATTHEW, MARK, AND JOHN
Christ walks on the sea .... Matthew 14:25
Mark 6:48
John 6:19

REPORTED BY ALL THE GOSPLES
The Feeding of the five thousand .... Matthew 14:15
Mark 6:34
Luke 9:10
John 6:1-14

Adapted from The Zondervan Pictorial Encyclopedia of the Bible, Volume 3, p. 580.
Merril C. Tenney, Editor. The Zondervan Corp. 1975; Grand Rapids.

HIS WILLINGNESS TO DIE

Sacrifice and offering thou didst not desire; mine ears hast thou opened: burnt offering and sin offering hast thou not required.

Then said I, Lo, I come: in the volume of the book it is written of me,

I delight to do thy will, O my God: yea, thy law is within my heart.

Psalm 40:6-8

Wherefore when he cometh into the world, he saith, Sacrifice and offering thou wouldest not, but a body hast thou prepared me:

In burnt offerings and sacrifices for sin thou hast had no pleasure.

Then said I, Lo, I come (in the volume of the book it is written of me,) to do thy will, O God.

Above when he said, Sacrifice and offering and burnt offerings and offering for sin thou wouldest not, neither hadst pleasure therein; which are offered by the law;

Then said he, Lo, I come to do thy will, O God. He taketh away the first, that he may establish the second.

By the which will we are sanctified through the offering of the body of Jesus Christ once for all.

Hebrews 10:5-10

Surely he hath borne our griefs, and carried our sorrows: yet we did esteem him stricken, smitten of God, and afflicted.

But he was wounded for our transgressions, he was bruised for our iniquities: the chastisement of our peace was upon him; and with his stripes we are healed.

All we like sheep have gone astray; we have turned every one to his own way; and the LORD hath laid on him the iniquity of us all.

Isaiah 53:4-6

Jesus saith unto them, My meat is to do the will of him that sent me, and to finish his work.

John 4:34

*   *   *   *

And after threescore and two weeks shall Messiah be cut off, but not for himself: and the people of the prince that shall come shall destroy the city and the sanctuary; and the end thereof shall be with a flood, and unto the end of the war desolations are determined.

Daniel 9:26

Who gave himself for us, that he might redeem us from all iniquity, and purify unto himself a peculiar people, zealous of good works.

Titus 2:14

Because for thy sake I have borne reproach; shame hath covered my face.

Psalm 69:7

All that pass by the way spoil him: he is a reproach to his neighbours.

Thou hast set up the right hand of his adversaries; thou hast made all his enemies to rejoice.

Thou hast also turned the edge of his sword, and hast not made him to stand in the battle.

Thou hast made his glory to cease, and cast his throne down to the ground.

The days of his youth hast thou shortened: thou hast covered him with shame. Selah.

How long, LORD? wilt thou hide thyself for ever? shall thy wrath burn like fire?

Remember how short my time is: wherefore hast thou made all men in vain?

What man is he that liveth, and shall not see death? shall he deliver his soul from the hand of the grave? Selah.

LORD, where are thy former loving-kindnesses, which thou swarest unto David in thy truth?

Remember, LORD, the reproach of thy servants; how I do bear in my bosom the reproach of all the mighty people;

Wherewith thine enemies have reproached, O LORD; wherewith they have reproached the footsteps of thine anointed.

Psalm 89:41-51

For even Christ pleased not himself; but, as it is written,

152

The reproaches of them that reproached thee fell on me.

* * * *

Therefore will I divide him a portion with the great, and he shall divide the spoil with the strong; because he hath poured out his soul unto death: and he was numbered with the transgressors; and he bare the sin of many, and made intercession for the transgressors.

Isaiah 53:12

I am the good shepherd: the good shepherd giveth his life for the sheep.

And other sheep I have, which are not of this fold: them also I must bring, and they shall hear my voice; and there shall be one fold, and one shepherd.

Therefore doth my Father love me, because I lay down my life, that I might take it again.

No man taketh it from me, but I lay it down of myself. I have power to lay it down, and I have power to take it again. This commandment have I received of my Father.

John 10:11, 16-18

Greater love hath no man than this, that a man lay down his life for his friends.

John 15:13

For ye know the grace of our LORD Jesus Christ, that, though he was rich, yet for your sakes he became poor, that ye through his poverty might be rich.

2 Corinthians 8:9

Who gave himself for our sins, that he might deliver us from this present evil world, according to the will of God and our Father.

Galatians 1:4

HIS SUFFERINGS

Who hath believed our report? and to whom is the arm of the LORD revealed?

Isaiah 53:1

But though he had done so many miracles before them, yet they believed not on him:

That the saying of Esaias the prophet might be fulfilled, which he spake, LORD, who hath believed our report? and to whom hath the arm of the LORD been revealed?

John 12:37, 38

Behold my servant, whom I have chosen; my beloved, in whom my soul is well pleased: I will put my spirit upon him, and he shall shew judgment to the Gentiles.

Matthew 12:18

But made himself of no reputation, and took upon him the form of a servant, and was made in the likeness of men.

Philippians 2:7

* * * *

But he was wounded for our transgressions, he was bruised for our iniquities: the chastisement of our peace was upon him; and with his stripes we are healed.

Isaiah 53:5

And one shall say unto him, What are these wounds in thine hands? Then he shall answer, Those with which I was wounded in the house of my friends.

Zechariah 13:6

For he hath made him to be sin for us, who knew no sin; that we might be made the righteousness of God in him.

2 Corinthians 5:21

* * * *

I gave my back to the smiters, and my cheeks to them that plucked off the hair: I hid not my face from shame and spitting.

Isaiah 50:6

Now gather thyself in troops, O daughter of troops: he hath laid siege against us: they shall smite the judge of Israel with a rod upon the cheek.

Micah 5:1

Then did they spit in his face, and buffeted him; and others smote him with the palms of their hands.

Matthew 26:67

And the men that held Jesus mocked him, and smote him.

Luke 22:63

All they that see me laugh me to scorn: they shoot out the lip, they shake the head, saying,

He trusted on the LORD that he would deliver him: let him deliver him, seeing he delighted in him.

Psalm 22:7, 8

And after that they had mocked him, they took the robe off from him, and put his own raiment on him, and led him away to crucify him.

Matthew 27:31

*   *   *   *

My knees are weak through fasting; and my flesh faileth of fatness.

I became also a reproach unto them: when they looked upon me they shaked their heads.

Psalm 109:24, 25

And he bearing his cross went forth into a place called the place of a skull, which is called in the Hebrew Golgotha. . .

John 19:17

And after that they had mocked him, they took the robe off from him, and put his own raiment on him, and led him away to crucify him.

And as they came out, they found a man of Cyrene, Simon by name: him they compelled to bear his cross.

Matthew 27:31, 32

For dogs have compassed me: the assembly of the wicked have inclosed me: they pierced my hands and my feet.

Psalms 22:16

And I will pour upon the house of David, and upon the inhabitants of Jerusalem, the spirit of grace and of supplications: and they shall look upon me whom they have pierced, and they shall mourn for him, as one mourneth for his only son, and shall be in bitterness for him, as one that is in bitterness for his firstborn.

Zechariah 12:10

And when they were come to the place, which is called Calvary, there they crucified him, and the malefactors, one on the right hand, and the other on the left.

Luke 23:33

The other disciples therefore said unto him, We have seen the LORD. But he said unto them, Except I shall see in his hands the print of the nails, and put my finger into the print of the nails, and thrust my hand into his side, I will not believe.

John 20:25

* * * *

I may tell all my bones: they look and stare upon me.

Psalm 22:17

And the people stood beholding. And the rulers also with them derided him, saying, He saved others; let him save himself, if he be Christ, the chosen of God.

Luke 23:35

* * * *

They part my garments among them, and cast lots upon my vesture.

Psalm 22:18

Then the soldiers, when they had crucified Jesus, took his garments, and made four parts, to every soldier a part; and also his coat: now the coat was without seam, woven from the top throughout.

They said therefore among themselves, Let us not rend it, but cast lots for it, whose it shall be: that the scripture might be fulfilled, which saith, They parted my raiment among them,

156

and for my vesture they did cast lots. These things therefore the
soldiers did.

John 19:23, 24

And they crucified him, and parted his garments, casting
lots: that it might be fulfilled which was spoken by the prophet,
They parted my garments among them, and upon my vesture
did they cast lots.

Matthew 27:35

And when they had crucified him, they parted his garments, casting lots upon them, what every man should take.

Mark 15:24

Then said Jesus, Father, forgive them; for they know not
what they do. And they parted his raiment, and cast lots.

Luke 23:34

*   *   *   *

They gave me also gall for my meat; and in my thirst they
gave me vinegar to drink

Psalm 69:21

My strength is dried up like a potsherd; and my tongue
cleaveth to my jaws; and thou hast brought me into the dust of
death.

Psalm 22:15

After this, Jesus knowing that all things were now accomplished, that the scripture might be fulfilled, saith, I
thirst.
Now there was set a vessel full of vinegar: and they filled a
spunge with vinegar, and put it upon hyssop, and put it to his
mouth.

John 19:28, 29

They gave him vinegar to drink mingled with gall: and
when he had tasted thereof, he would not drink.

Matthew 27:34

My God, my god, why hast thou forsaken me? why art
thou so far from helping me, and from the words of my roaring?

Psalm 22:1

157

And about the ninth hour Jesus cried with a loud voice, saying, Eli, Eli, lama sabach-thani? that is to say, My God, my God, why hast thou forsaken me?

Matthew 27:46

* * * *

I am poured out like water, and all my bones are out of joint: my heart is like wax; it is melted in the midst of my bowels.

Psalm 22:14

And I will pour upon the house of David, and upon the inhabitants of Jerusalem, the spirit of grace and of supplications: and they shall look upon me whom they have pierced.

Zechariah 12:10

But one of the soldiers with a spear pierced his side, and forthwith came there out blood and water.

John 19:34

* * * *

Yet it pleased the LORD to bruise him; he hath put him to grief: when thou shalt make his soul an offering for sin, he shall see his seed, he shall prolong his days, and the pleasure of the LORD shall prosper in his hand.

Therefore will I divide him a portion with the great, and he shall divide the spoil with the strong; because he hath poured out his soul unto death: and he was numbered with the transgressors; and he bare the sin of many, and made intercession for the transgressors.

Isaiah 53:10-12

For I say unto you, that this that is written must yet be accomplished in me, And he was reckoned among the transgressors: for the things concerning me have an end.

Luke 22:37

* * * *

But in mine adversity they rejoiced, and gathered themselves together: yea, the abjects gathered themselves together against me, and I knew it not; they did tear me, and ceased not:

With hypocritical mockers in feasts, they gnashed upon me with their teeth.

Psalm 35:15, 16

Then the soldiers of the governor took Jesus into the common hall, and gathered unto him the whole band of soldiers.

And they stripped him, and put on him a scarlet robe.

And when they had platted a crown of thorns, they put it upon his head, and a reed in his right hand: and they bowed the knee before him, and mocked him, saying, Hail, King of the Jews!

And they spit upon him, and took the reed, and smote him on the head.

Matthew 27:27-30

* * * *

Thou hast known my reproach, and my shame, and my dishonour: mine adversaries are all before thee.

Psalm 69:19

Looking unto Jesus the author and finisher of our faith; who for the joy that was set before him endured the cross, despising the shame, and is set down at the right hand of the throne of God.

Hebrews 12:2

Christ hath redeemed us from the curse of the law, being made a curse for us: for it is written, Cursed is every one that hangeth on a tree.

Galatians 3:13

HIS OFFER OF SALVATION

Behold, the LORD God will help me; who is he that shall condemn me? lo, they all shall wax old as a garment; the moth shall eat them up.

Isaiah 50:9

There is therefore now no condemnation to them which are in Christ Jesus, who walk not after the flesh, but after the Spirit.

Who is he that condemneth? It is Christ that died, yea rather, that is risen again, who is even at the right hand of God, who also maketh intercession for us.

Romans 8:1, 34

He that believeth on him is not condemned: but he that believeth not is condemned already, because he hath not believed in the name of the only begotten Son of God.

John 3:18

Verily, verily, I say unto you, He that heareth my word, and believeth on him that sent me, hath everlasting life, and shall not come into condemnation; but is passed from death unto life.

John 5:24

* * * *

The LORD thy God in the midst of thee is mighty; he will save, he will rejoice over thee with joy; he will rest in his love, he will joy over thee with singing.

Zephaniah 3:17

For the Son of man is come to seek and to save that which was lost.

Luke 19:10

And she shall bring forth a son, and thou shalt call his name JESUS: for he shall save his people from their sins.

Matthew 1:21

This is a faithful saying, and worthy of all acceptation, that Christ Jesus came into the world to save sinners; of whom I am chief.

1 Timothy 1:15

For the Son of man is come to save that which was lost.

Matthew 18:11

And said unto them, Thus it is written, and thus it behoved Christ to suffer, and to rise from the dead the third day:

And that repentance and remission of sins should be preached in his name among all nations, beginning at Jerusalem.

Luke 24:46, 47

For therefore we both labour and suffer reproach, because we trust in the living God, who is the Saviour of all men, specially of those that believe.

1 Timothy 4:10

That if thou shalt confess with thy mouth the LORD Jesus, and shalt believe in thine heart that God hath raised him from the dead, thou shalt be saved.

For with the heart man believeth unto righteousness; and with the mouth confession is made unto salvation.

Romans 10:9, 10

*　*　*　*

But the salvation of the righteous is of the LORD: he is their strength in the time of trouble.

Psalm 37:39

Wherefore lay apart all filthiness and superfluity of naughtiness, and receive with meekness the engrafted word, which is able to save your souls.

James 1:21

*　*　*　*

And he said, It is a light thing that thou shouldest be my servant to raise up the tribes of Jacob, and to restore the preserved of Israel: I will also give thee for a light to the Gentiles, that thou mayest be my salvation unto the end of the earth.

Isaiah 49:6

The people that walked in darkness have seen a great

light: they that dwell in the land of the shadow of death, upon them hath the light shined.

Isaiah 9:2

The LORD is my light and my salvation; whom shall I fear? the LORD is the strength of my life; of whom shall I be afraid?

Psalm 27:1

The people which sat in darkness saw great light; and to them which sat in the region and shadow of death light is sprung up.

From that time Jesus began to preach, and to say, Repent: for the kingdom of heaven is at hand.

Matthew 4:16, 17

And all flesh shall see the salvation of God.

Luke 3:6

Therefore as by the offence of one judgment came upon all men to condemnation; even so by the righteousness of one the free gift came upon all men unto justification of life.

Romans 5:18

* * * *

And it shall be said in that day, Lo, this is our God; we have waited for him, and he will save us: this is the LORD; we have waited for him, we will be glad and rejoice in his salvation.

Isaiah 25:9

And it shall come to pass, that whosoever shall call on the name of the LORD shall be saved.

Acts 2:21

* * * *

Behold, God is my salvation; I will trust, and not be afraid: for the LORD JEHOVAH is my strength and my song; he also is become my salvation.

Isaiah 12:2

And they sung a new song, saying, Thou art worthy to take the book, and to open the seals thereof: for thou wast

162

slain, and hast redeemed us to God by thy blood out of every kindred, and tongue, and people, and nation;

And hast made us unto our God kings and priests: and we shall reign on the earth.

Revelation 5:9, 10

* * * *

The God of my rock; in him will I trust: he is my shield, and the horn of my salvation, my high tower, and my refuge, my saviour; thou savest me from violence.

2 Samuel 22:3

And when he had removed him, he raised up unto them David to be their king; to whom also he gave testimony, and said, I have found David the son of Jesse, a man after mine own heart, which shall fulfil all my will.

Of this man's seed hath God according to his promise raised unto Israel a Saviour, Jesus.

Acts 13:22, 23

And hath raised up an horn of salvation for us in the house of his servant David;

As he spake by the mouth of his holy prophets, which have been since the world began.

Luke 1:69, 70

* * * *

Mercy and truth are met together; righteousness and peace have kissed each other.

Psalm 85:10

Peace I leave with you, my peace I give unto you: not as the world giveth, give I unto you. Let not your heart be troubled, neither let it be afraid.

John 14:27

Therefore being justified by faith, we have peace with God through our LORD Jesus Christ.

Romans 5:1

But Israel shall be saved in the LORD with an everlasting

salvation: ye shall not be ashamed nor confounded world without end.

Isaiah 45:17

And so all Israel shall be saved: as it is written, There shall come out of Sion the Deliverer, and shall turn away ungodliness from Jacob:

For this is my covenant unto them, when I shall take away their sins.

Romans 11:26, 27

For this is the covenant that I will make with the house of Israel after those days, saith the LORD; I will put my laws into their mind, and write them in their hearts: and I will be to them, a God, and they shall be to me a people.

Hebrews 8:10

* * * *

With long life will I satisfy him, and shew him my salvation.

Psalm 91:16

He that believeth and is baptized shall be saved; but he that believeth not shall be damned.

Mark 16:16

Behold, I stand at the door, and knock: if any man hear my voice, and open the door, I will come in to him, and will sup with him, and he with me.

Revelation 3:20

For God so loved the world, that he gave his only begotten Son, that whosoever believeth in him should not perish, but have everlasting life.

John 3:16

HIS JUSTICE

The God of Israel said, the Rock of Israel spake to me, He that ruleth over men must be just, ruling in the fear of God.

2 Samuel 23:13

Rejoice greatly, O daughter of Zion; shout, O daughter of Jerusalem: behold, thy King cometh unto thee: he is just, and having salvation; lowly, and riding upon an ass, and upon a colt the foal of an ass.

Zechariah 9:9

When he was set down on the judgment seat, his wife sent unto him, saying, Have thou nothing to do with that just man: for I have suffered many things this day in a dream because of him.

Matthew 27:19

I can of mine own self do nothing: as I hear, I judge: and my judgment is just; because I seek not mine own will, but the will of the Father which hath sent me.

John 5:30

* * * *

For the LORD is our judge, the LORD is our lawgiver, the LORD is our king; he will save us.

Isaiah 33:22

I charge thee therefore before God, and the LORD Jesus Christ, who shall judge the quick and the dead at his appearing and his kingdom.

2 Timothy 4:1

I can of mine own self do nothing: as I hear, I judge: and my judgment is just; because I seek not mine own will, but the will of the Father which hath sent me.

John 5:30

HIS RIGHTEOUSNESS

O LORD God of Israel, thou art righteous: for we remain yet escaped, as it is this day: behold, we are before thee in our trespasses: for we cannot stand before thee because of this.

Ezra 9:15

Thou lovest righteousness, and hatest wickedness: therefore God, thy God, hath anointed thee with the oil of gladness above thy fellows.

Psalm 45:7

Thou hast loved righteousness, and hated iniquity; therefore God, even thy God, hath anointed thee with the oil of gladness above thy fellows.

Hebrews 1:9

* * * *

But with righteousness shall he judge the poor, and reprove with equity for the meek of the earth: and he shall smite the earth with the rod of his mouth, and with the breath of his lips shall he slay the wicked.

And righteousness shall be the girdle of his loins, and faithfulness the girdle of his reins.

Isaiah 11:4, 5

And I saw thrones, and they sat upon them, and judgment was given unto them: and I saw the souls of them that were beheaded for the witness of Jesus, and for the word of God, and which had not worshipped the beast, neither his image, neither had received his mark upon their foreheads, or in their hands; and they lived and reigned with Christ a thousand years.

Revelation 20:4

And the third angel poured out his vial upon the rivers and fountains of waters; and they became blood.

And I heard the angel of the waters say, Thou art righteous, O LORD, which art, and wast, and shalt be, because thou hast judged thus.

For they have shed the blood of saints and prophets, and thou hast given them blood to drink; for they are worthy.

Revelation 16:4-6

* * * *

Behold, a king shall reign in righteousness, and princes shall rule in judgment.

Isaiah 32:1

And after these things I heard a great voice of much people in heaven, saying, Alleluia; Salvation, and glory, and honour, and power, unto the LORD our God:

For true and righteous are his judgments: for he hath judged the great whore, which did corrupt the earth with her fornification, and hath avenged the blood of his servants at her hand.

Revelation 19:1, 2

*   *   *   *

Behold my servant, whom I uphold; mine elect, in whom my soul delighteth; I have put my spirit upon him: he shall bring forth judgment to the Gentiles.

Isaiah 42:1

The LORD is well pleased for his righteousness' sake; he will magnify the law, and make it honourable.

Isaiah 42:21

The God of Abraham, and of Isaac, and of Jacob, the God of our fathers, hath glorified his Son Jesus; whom ye delivered up, and denied him in the presence of Pilate, when he was determined to let him go.

But ye denied the Holy One and the Just, and desired a murderer to be granted unto you;

Acts 3:13, 14

*   *   *   *

Thou art the LORD the God, who didst choose Abram, and broughtest him forth out of Ur of the Chaldees, and gavest him the name of Abraham;

And foundest his heart faithful before thee, and madest a covenant with him to give the land of the Canaanites, the Hittites, the Amorites, and the Perizzites, and the Jebusites, and the Girgashites, to give it, I say, to his seed, and hast performed thy words; for thou art righteous.

Nehemiah 9:7, 8

Whom God hath set forth to be a propitiation through faith in his blood, to declare his righteousness for the remission of sins that are past, through the forbearance of God.

Romans 3:25

For the promise, that he should be the heir of the world, was not to Abraham, or to his seed, through the law, but through the righteousness of faith.

Romans 4:13

For he hath made him to be sin for us, who knew no sin; that we might be made the righteousness of God in him.

2 Corinthians 5:21

* * * *

Behold, the days come, saith the LORD, that I will raise unto David a righteous Branch, and a King shall reign and prosper, and shall execute judgment and justice in the earth.

In his days Judah shall be saved, and Israel shall dwell safely: and this is his name whereby he shall be called, THE LORD OUR RIGHTEOUSNESS.

Jeremiah 23:5, 6

The just LORD is in the midst thereof; he will not do iniquity: every morning doth he bring his judgment to light, he faileth not; but the unjust knoweth no shame.

Zephaniah 3:5

And I heard the angel of the waters say, Thou art righteousness, O LORD, which art, and wast, and shalt be, because thou hast judged thus.

For they have shed the blood of saints and prophets, and thou hast given them blood to drink; for they are worthy.

Revelation 16:5, 6

* * * *

Oh let the wickedness of the wicked come to an end; but establish the just: for the righteous God trieth the hearts and reins.

My defence is of God, which saveth the upright in heart.

God judgeth the righteous, and God is angry with the wicked every day.

Psalm 7:9-11

For God is not unrighteous to forget your work and labour of love, which ye have shewed toward his name, in that ye have ministered to the saints, and do minister.

Hebrews 6:10

*   *   *   *

Many a time have they afflicted me from my youth, may Israel now say:

Many a time have they afflicted me from my youth: yet they have not prevailed against me.

The plowers plowed upon my back: they made long their furrows.

The LORD is righteous: he hath cut asunder the cords of the wicked.

Psalm 129:1-4

O sing unto the LORD a new song; for he hath done marvellous things: his right hand, and his holy arm, hath gotten him the victory.

The LORD hath made known his salvation: his righteousness hath he openly shewed in the sight of the heathen.

He hath remembered his mercy and his truth toward the house of Israel: all the ends of the earth have seen the salvation of our God.

Psalm 98:1-3

Seeing it is a righteous thing with God to recompense tribulation to them that trouble you.

And to you who are troubled rest with us, when the LORD Jesus shall be revealed from heaven with his mighty angels.

2 Thessalonians 1:6, 7

HIS PRIESTHOOD

The LORD hath sworn, and will not repent, Thou art a priest for ever after the order of Melchizedek.

Psalm 110:4

And speak unto him, saying, Thus speaketh the LORD of hosts, saying, Behold the man whose name is The BRANCH; and he shall grow up out of his place, and he shall build the temple of the LORD:

Even he shall build the temple of the LORD; and he shall bear the glory, and shall sit and rule upon his throne; and he shall be a priest upon his throne: and the counsel of peace shall be between them both.

Zechariah 6:12, 13

Wherefore, holy brethren, partakers of the heavenly calling, consider the Apostle and High Priest of our profession, Christ Jesus.

Hebrews 3:1

For every high priest taken from among men is ordained for men in things pertaining to God, that he may offer both gifts and sacrifices for sins:

Who can have compassion on the ignorant, and on them that are out of the way; for that he himself also is compassed with infirmity.

And by reason hereof he ought, as for the people, so also for himself, to offer for sins.

And no man taketh this honour unto himself, but he that is called of God, as was Aaron.

So also Christ glorified not himself to be made an high priest; but he that said unto him, Thou art my Son, to day have I begotten thee.

As he saith also in another place, Thou art a priest for ever after the order of Melchisedec.

Hebrews 5:1-6

Whither the forerunner is for us entered, even Jesus, made an high priest for ever after the order of Melchisedec.

Hebrews 6:20

Now of the things which we have spoken this is the sum: We have such an high priest, who is set on the right hand of the throne of the Majesty in the heavens.

Hebrews 8:1

But Christ being come an high priest of good things to come, by a greater and more perfect tabernacle, not made with hands, that is to say, not of this building.

Hebrews 9:11

And having an high priest over the house of God.

Hebrews 10:21

*   *   *   *

And if a soul sin, and commit any of these things which are forbidden to be done by the commandments of the LORD; though he wist it not, yet is he guilty, and shall bear his iniquity.

And he shall bring a ram without blemish out of the flock, with thy estimation, for a trespass offering, unto the priest: and the priest shall make an atonement for him concerning his ignorance wherein he erred and wist it not, and it shall be forgiven him.

Leviticus 5:17, 18

Wherefore in all things it behoved him to be made like unto his brethren, that he might be a merciful and faithful high priest in things pertaining to God, to make reconciliation for the sins of the people.

Hebrews 2:17

Seeing then that we have a great high priest, that is passed into the heavens, Jesus the Son of God, let us hold fast our profession.

For we have not an high priest which cannot be touched with the feeling of our infirmities; but was in all points tempted like as we are, yet without sin.

Hebrews 4:14, 15

For such an high priest became us, who is holy, harmless, undefiled, separate from sinners, and made higher than the heavens;

Who needeth not daily, as those high priests, to offer up sacrifice, first for his own sins, and then for the people's: for this he did once, when he offered up himself.

Hebrews 7:26, 27

How much more shall the blood of Christ, who through the eternal Spirit offered himself without spot to God, purge your conscience from dead works to serve the living God?

Hebrews 9:14

172

HIS EXALTATION

The adversaries of the LORD shall be broken to pieces; out of heaven shall he thunder upon them: the LORD shall judge the ends of the earth; and he shall give strength unto his king, and exalt the horn of his anointed.

1 Samuel 2:10

When the Son of man shall come in his glory, and all the holy angels with him, then shall he sit upon the throne of his glory:

And before him shall be gathered all nations: and he shall separate them one from another, as a shepherd divideth his sheep from the goats:

Then shall the King say unto them on his right hand, Come, ye blessed of my Father, inherit the kingdom prepared for you from the foundation of the world.

Matthew 25:31, 32, 34

*   *   *   *

For thou art the glory of their strength: and in thy favour our horn shall be exalted.

But my faithfulness and my mercy shall be with him: and in my name shall his horn be exalted.

Psalm 89:17, 24

But my horn shalt thou exalt like the horn of an unicorn: I shall be anointed with fresh oil.

Let them praise the name of the LORD: for his name alone is excellent; his glory is above the earth and heaven.

Psalm 92:10; 148:13

And again, when he bringeth in the first-begotten into the world, he saith, And let all the angels of God worship him.

Hebrews 1:6

And when he had taken the book, the four beasts and four and twenty elders fell down before the Lamb, having every one of them harps, and golden vials full of odours, which are the prayers of saints.

Revelation 5:8

Which he wrought in Christ, when he raised him from the dead, and set him at his own right hand in the heavenly places,

Far above all principality, and power, and might, and dominion, and every name that is named, not only in this world, but also in that which is to come.

Ephesians 1:20, 21

For Christ is not entered into the holy places made with hands, which are the figures of the true; but into heaven itself, now to appear in the presence of God for us.

Hebrews 9:24

Who is gone into heaven, and is on the right hand of God; angels and authorities and powers being made subject unto him.

1 Peter 3:22

* * * *

His glory is great in thy salvation: honour and majesty hast thou laid upon him.

Their fruit shalt thou destroy from the earth, and their seed from among the children of men.

For they intended evil against thee: they imagined a mischievous device, which they are not able to perform.

Therefore shalt thou make them turn their back, when thou shalt make ready thine arrows upon thy strings against the face of them.

Psalm 21:5, 10-12

Wherefore God also hath highly exalted him, and given him a name which is above every name.

Philippians 2:9

* * * *

But the LORD of hosts shall be exalted in judgment, and God that is holy shall be sanctified in righteousness.

Isaiah 5:16

Saying with a loud voice, Fear God, and give glory to him; for the hour of his judgment is come: and worship him that made heaven, and earth, and the sea, and the fountains of waters.

Revelation 14:7

Who shalt not fear thee, O LORD, and glorify thy name? for thou only art holy: for all nations shall come and worship before thee; for thy judgments are made manifest.

Revelation 15:4

And I fell at his feet to worship him. And he said unto me, See thou do it not: I am thy fellowservant, and of thy brethren that have the testimony of Jesus: worship God: for the testimony of Jesus is the spirit of prophecy.

And I saw heaven opened, and behold a white horse; and he that sat upon him was called Faithful and True, and in righteousness he doth judge and make war.

His eyes were as a flame of fire, and on his head were many crowns; and he had a name written, that no man knew, but he himself.

Revelation 19:10-12

* * * *

O magnify the LORD with me, and let us exalt his name together.

Psalm 34:3

And Mary said, My soul doth magnify the LORD.

Luke 1:46

* * * *

The LORD is my strength and song, and he is become my salvation: he is my God, and I will prepare him an habitation; my father's God, and I will exalt him.

Exodus 15:2

Saying with a loud voice, Worthy is the Lamb that was slain to receive power, and riches, and wisdom, and strength, and honour, and glory, and blessing.

And every creature which is in heaven, and on the earth, and under the earth, and such as are in the sea, and all that are in them, heard I saying, Blessing, and honour, and glory, and power, be unto him that sitteth upon the throne, and unto the Lamb for ever and ever.

Revelation 5:12, 13

HIS COMING GLORY
AND POWER

The LORD said unto my LORD, Sit thou at my right hand, until I make thine enemies thy footstool.

Psalm 110:1

Who being the brightness of his glory, and the express image of his person, and upholding all things by the word of his power, when he had by himself purged our sins, sat down on the right hand of the Majesty on high.

Hebrews 1:3

So then after the LORD had spoken unto them, he was received up into heaven, and sat on the right hand of God.

Mark 16:19

For David is not ascended into the heavens: but he saith himself, The LORD said unto my LORD, Sit thou on my right hand,
Until I make thy foes thy footstool.

Acts 2:34, 35

* * * *

But who may abide the day of his coming? and who shall stand when he appeareth? for he is like a refiner's fire, and like fullers' soap:
And he shall sit as a refiner and purifier of silver: and he shall purify the sons of Levi, and purge them as gold and silver, that they may offer unto the LORD, an offering in righteousness.

Malachi 3:2, 3

And the kings of the earth, and the great men, and the rich men, and the chief captains, and the mighty men, and every bondman, and every free man, hid themselves in the dens and in the rocks of the mountains;
And said to the mountains and rocks, Fall on us, and hide us from the face of him that sitteth on the throne, and from the wrath of the Lamb:

For the great day of his wrath is come; and who shall be able to stand?

Revelation 6:15-17

* * * *

But unto you that fear my name shall the Sun of righteousness arise with healing in his wings; and ye shall go forth, and grow up as calves of the stall.

Malachi 4:2

And Jesus said, I am: and ye shall see the Son of man sitting on the right hand of power, and coming in the clouds of heaven.

Mark 14:62

Who is gone into heaven, and is on the right hand of God; angels and authorities and powers being made subject unto him.

1 Peter 3:22

And Enoch also, the seventh from Adam, prophesied of these, saying, Behold, the LORD cometh with ten thousands of his saints,

To execute judgment upon all, and to convince all that are ungodly among them of all their ungodly deeds which they have ungodly committed, and of all their hard speeches which ungodly sinners have spoken against him.

Jude 14, 15

* * * *

Behold, thou shalt call a nation that thou knowest not, and nations that knew not thee shall run unto thee because of the LORD thy God, and for the Holy One of Israel; for he hath glorified thee.

Isaiah 55:5

I am he that liveth, and was dead; and, behold, I am alive for evermore, Amen; and have the keys of hell and of death.

Revelation 1:18

And from Jesus Christ, who is the faithful witness, and

the first begotten of the dead, and the prince of the kings of the earth. Unto him that loved us, and washed us from our sins, in his own blood.

And hath made us kings and priests unto God and his Father; to him be glory and dominion for ever and ever. Amen.

Behold, he cometh with clouds; and every eye shall see him, and they also which pierced him: and all kindreds of the earth shall wail because of him. Even so, Amen.

Revelation 1:5-7

* * * *

And he shall judge among many people, and rebuke strong nations afar off; and they shall beat their swords into plowshares, and their spears into pruninghooks: nation shall not lift up a sword against nation, neither shall they learn war any more.

Micah 4:3

For the earth shall be filled with the knowledge of the glory of the LORD, as the waters cover the sea.

Habakkuk 2:14

And I will shake all nations, and the desire of all nations shall come: and I will fill this house with glory, saith the LORD of hosts.

The silver is mine, and the gold is mine, saith the LORD of hosts.

The glory of this latter house shall be greater than of the former, saith the LORD of hosts: and in this place will I give peace, saith the LORD of hosts.

Haggai 2:7-9

And it shall be in that day, that living waters shall go out from Jerusalem; half of them toward the former sea, and half of them toward the hinder sea: in summer and in winter shall it be.

And the LORD shall be king over all the earth: in that day shall there be one LORD, and his name one.

Zechariah 14:8, 9

178

Wherefore God also hath highly exalted him, and given him a name which is above every name:

That at the name of Jesus every knee should bow, of things in heaven, and things in earth, and things under the earth;

And that every tongue should confess that Jesus Christ is LORD, to the glory of God the Father.

Philippians 2:9-11

And he shewed me a pure river of water of life, clear as crystal, proceeding out of the throne of God and of the Lamb.

In the midst of the street of it, and on either side of the river, was there the tree of life, which bare twelve manner of fruits, and yielded her fruit every month: and the leaves of the tree were for the healing of the nations.

And there shall be no more curse: but the throne of God and of the Lamb shall be in it; and his servants shall serve him:

And they shall see his face; and his name shall be in their foreheads.

And there shall be no night there; and they need no candle, neither light of the sun; for the LORD God giveth them light: and they shall reign for ever and ever.

Revelation 22:1-5

* * * *

I saw in the night visions, and, behold, one like the Son of man came with the clouds of heaven, and came to the Ancient of days, and they brought him near before him,

And there was given him dominion, and glory, and a kingdom, that all people, nations, and languages, should serve him: his dominion is an everlasting dominion, which shall not pass away, and his kingdom that which shall not be destroyed.

Daniel 7:13, 14

Jesus saith unto him, Thou hast said: nevertheless I say unto you, Hereafter shall ye see the Son of man sitting on the right hand of power, and coming in the clouds of heaven.

Matthew 26:64

HIS CREATIVE WORK

And God said, Let us make man in our image, after our likeness: and let them have dominion over the fish of the sea, and over the fowl of the air, and over the cattle, and over all the earth, and over every creeping thing that creepeth upon the earth.

Genesis 1:26

Praise ye him, all his angels: praise ye him, all his hosts.

Praise ye him, sun and moon: praise him, all ye stars of light.

Praise him, ye heavens of heavens, and ye waters that be above the heavens.

Let them praise the name of the LORD: for he commanded, and they were created.

Psalm 148:2-5

The LORD hath made all things for himself: yea, even the wicked for the day of evil.

Proverbs 16:4

For by him were all things created, that are in heaven, and that are in earth, visible and invisible, whether they be thrones, or dominions, or principalities, or powers: all things were created by him, and for him.

Colossians 1:16

Thou art worthy, O LORD, to receive glory and honour and power: for thou hast created all things, and for thy pleasure they are and were created.

Revelation 4:11

* * * *

I said, O my God, take me not away in the midst of my days: thy years are throughout all generations.

Of old hast thou laid the foundation of the earth: and the heavens are the work of thy hands.

They shall perish, but thou shalt endure: yea, all them shall wax old like a garment; as a vesture shalt thou change them, and they shall be changed:

But thou art the same, and thy years shall have no end.

Psalm 102:24-27

But unto the Son he saith, Thy throne, O God, is for ever and ever: a sceptre of righteousness is the sceptre of thy kingdom.

And, Thou, LORD, in the beginning hast laid the foundation of the earth; and the heavens are the works of thine hands:

They shall perish; but thou remainest; and they all shall wax old as doth a garment;

And as a vesture shalt thou fold them up, and they shall be changed: but thou art the same, and thy years shall not fail.

Hebrews 1:8, 10-12

Hast thou not known? Hast thou not heard, that the everlasting God, the LORD, the Creator of the ends of the earth, fainteth not, neither is weary? there is no searching of his understanding.

Isaiah 40:28

All things were made by him; and without him was not any thing made that was made.

John 1:3

* * * *

Thou, even thou, art LORD alone; thou hast made heaven, the heaven of heavens, with all their host, the earth, and all things that are therein, the seas, and all that is therein, and thou preservest them all; and the host of heaven worshippeth thee.

Nehemiah 9:6

And he is before all things, and by him all things consist.

Colossians 1:17

Who being the brightness of his glory, and the express image of his person, and upholding all things by the word of his power, when he had by himself purged our sins, sat down on the right hand of the Majesty on high.

Hebrews 1:3

HIS COMPASSION

He shall feed his flock like a shepherd: he shall gather the lambs with his arm, and carry them in his bosom, and shall gently lead those that are with young.

Isaiah 40:11

A bruised reed shall he not break, and the smoking flax shall he not quench: he shall bring forth judgment unto truth.

Isaiah 42:3

But when he saw the multitudes, he was moved with compassion on them, because they fainted, and were scattered abroad, as sheep having no shepherd.

Matthew 9:36

And Jesus, when he came out, saw much people, and was moved with compassion toward them, because they were as sheep not having a shepherd: and he began to teach them many things.

Mark 6:34

*　*　*　*

In all their affliction he was afflicted, and the angel of his presence saved them: in his love and in his pity he redeemed them; and he bare them, and carried them all the days of old.

Isaiah 63:9

And Jesus went forth, and saw a great multitude, and was moved with compassion toward them, and he healed their sick.

Matthew 14:14

Then Jesus called his disciples unto him, and said, I have compassion on the multitude, because they continue with me now three days, and have nothing to eat: and I will not send them away fasting, lest they faint in the way.

Matthew 15:32

So Jesus had compassion on them, and touched their eyes: and immediately their eyes received sight, and they followed him.

Matthew 20:34

*　*　*　*

Surely he hath borne our griefs, and carried our sorrows:
yet we did esteem him stricken, smitten of God, and afflicted.

Isaiah 53:4

When the even was come, they brought unto him many
that were possessed with devils: and he cast out the spirits with
his word, and healed all that were sick:

That it might be fulfilled which was spoken by Esaias the
prophet, saying, Himself took our infirmities, and bare our
sicknesses.

Matthew 8:16, 17

O Jerusalem, Jerusalem, thou that killest the prophets,
and stonest them which are sent unto thee, how often would I
have gathered thy children together, even as a hen gathereth her
chickens under her wings, and ye would not!

Matthew 23:37

I have compassion on the multitude, because they have
now been with me three days, and have nothing to eat.

Mark 8:2

And there came a leper to him, beseeching him, and kneel-
ing down to him, and saying unto him, If thou wilt, thou canst
make me clean.

And Jesus, moved with compassion, put forth his hand,
and touched him, and saith unto him, I will; be thou clean.

Mark 1:40, 41

* * * *

Therefore the showers have been withholden, and there
hath been no latter rain; and thou hadst a whore's forehead,
thou refusedst to be ashamed.

Wilt thou not from this time cry unto me, My father, thou
art the guide of my youth?

Jeremiah 3:3, 4

Then they that feared the LORD spake often one to
another: and the LORD hearkened, and heard it, and a book of
remembrance was written before him for them that feared the
LORD, and that thought upon his name.

And they shall be mine saith the LORD of hosts, in that

day when I make up my jewels; and I will spare them, as a man spareth his own son that serveth him.

Malachi 3:16, 17

When Jesus therefore saw her weeping, and the Jews also weeping which came with her, he groaned in the spirit, and was troubled,

And said, Where have ye laid him? They said unto him, Lord, come and see.

Jesus wept.

Then said the Jews, Behold how he loved him!

John 11:33-36

Now when he came nigh to the gate of the city, behold, there was a dead man carried out, the only son of his mother, and she was a widow: and much people of the city was with her.

And when the Lord saw her, he had compassion on her, and said unto her, Weep not.

And he came and touched the bier: and they that bare him stood still. And he said, Young man, I say unto thee, Arise.

And he that was dead sat up, and began to speak. And he delivered him to his mother.

Luke 7:12-15

HIS POWER

Who is this that cometh from Edom, with dyed garments from Bozrah? this that is glorious in his apparel, travelling in the greatness of his strength? I that speak in righteousness, mighty to save.

Wherefore art thou red in thine apparel, and thy garments like him that treadeth in the winefat?

I have trodden the winepress alone; and of the people there was none with me: for I will tread them in mine anger, and trample them in my fury; and their blood shall be sprinkled upon my garments, and I will stain all my raiment.

For the day of vengeance is in mine heart, and the year of my redeemed is come.

Isaiah 63:1-4

And the winepress was trodden without the city, and blood came out of the winepress, even unto the horse bridles, by the space of a thousand and six hundred furlongs.

Revelation 14:20

Who being the brightness of his glory, and the express image of his person, and upholding all things by the word of his power, when he had by himself purged our sins, sat down on the right hand of the Majesty on high.

Hebrews 1:3

And he was clothed with a vesture dipped in blood: and his name is called The Word of God.

Revelation 19:13

* * * *

Thine, O LORD, is the greatness, and the power, and the glory, and the victory, and the majesty: for all that is in the heaven and in the earth is thine; thine is the kingdom, O LORD, and thou art exalted as head above all.

1 Chronicles 29:11

And lead us not into temptation, but deliver us from evil: For thine is the kingdom, and the power, and the glory, for ever. Amen.

Matthew 6:13

And every creature which is in heaven, and on the earth, and under the earth, and such as are in the sea, and all that are in them, heard I saying, Blessing, and honour, and glory, and power, be unto him that sitteth upon the throne, and unto the Lamb for ever and ever.

Revelation 5:13

* * * *

I will ransom them from the power of the grave; I will redeem them from death: O death, I will be thy plagues; O grave, I will be thy destruction: repentance shall be hid from mine eyes.

Hosea 13:14

O death, where is thy sting? O grave, where is thy victory?

1 Corinthians 15:55

* * * *

Against thee, thee only, have I sinned, and done this evil in thy sight: that thou mightest be justified when thou speakest, and be clear when thou judgest.

Psalm 51:4

And, behold, they brought to him a man sick of the palsy, lying on a bed: and Jesus seeing their faith said unto the sick of the palsy; Son, be of good cheer; thy sins be forgiven thee.

But that ye may know that the Son of man hath power on earth to forgive sins, (then saith he to the sick of the palsy,) Arise, take up thy bed, and go to thine house.

Mathew 9:2,6

* * * *

Lift up your eyes on high, and behold who hath created these things, that bringeth out their host by number: he calleth them all by names by the greatness of his might, for that he is strong in power; not one faileth.

Isaiah 40:26

* * * *

God hath spoken once; twice have I heard this; that power belongeth unto God.

Psalm 62:11

And Jesus came and spake unto them, saying, All power is given unto me in heaven and in earth.

Matthew 28:18

And after these things I heard a great voice of much people in heaven, saying, Alleluia; Salvation, and glory, and honour, and power, unto the LORD our God.

Revelation 19:1

HIS HOLINESS

But the LORD of hosts shall be exalted in judgment, and God that is holy shall be sanctified in righteousness.

Isaiah 5:16

In the year that king Uzziah died I saw also the LORD sitting upon a throne, high and lifted up, and his train filled the temple.

Above it stood the seraphims: each one had six wings; with twain he covered his face, and with twain he covered his feet, and with twain he did fly.

And one cried unto another, and said, Holy, holy, holy, is the LORD of hosts: the whole earth is full of his glory.

Isaiah 6:1-3

But as he which hath called you is holy, so be ye holy in all manner of conversation;

Because it is written, Be ye holy; for I am holy.

1 Peter 1:15, 16

* * * *

Thou lovest righteousness, and hatest wickedness: therefore God, thy God, hath anointed thee with the oil of gladness above thy fellows.

Psalms 45:7

But unto the Son he saith, Thy throne, O God, is for ever and ever: a sceptre of righteousness is the sceptre of thy kingdom.

Thou hast loved righteousness, and hated iniquity; therefore God, even thy God, hath anointed thee with the oil of gladness above thy fellows.

Hebrews 1:8, 9

* * * *

For the LORD thy God walketh in the midst of thy camp, to deliver thee, and to give up thine enemies before thee; therefore shall thy camp be holy: that he see no unclean thing in thee, and turn away from thee.

Deuteronomy 23:14

For such an high priest became us, who is holy, harmless, undefiled, separate from sinners, and made higher than the heavens.

Hebrews 7:26

* * * *

Then thou spakest in vision to thy holy one, and saidst, I have laid help upon one that is mighty; I have exalted one chosen out of the people.

Psalm 89:19

For of a truth against thy holy child Jesus, whom thou hast anointed, both Herod, and Pontius Pilate, with the Gentiles, and the people of Israel, were gathered together,

By stretching forth thine hand to heal; and that signs and wonders may be done by the name of thy holy child Jesus.

Acts 4:27, 30

* * * *

Exalt ye the LORD our God, and worship at his footstool; for he is holy.

Exalt the LORD our God, and worship at his holy hill; for the LORD our God is holy.

Psalm 99:5, 9

And every man that hath this hope in him purifieth himself, even as he is pure.

1 John 3:3

* * * *

Cry out and shout, thou inhabitant of Zion: for great is the Holy One of Israel in the midst of thee.

Isaiah 12:6

Then said Jesus unto the twelve, Will ye also go away?

Then Simon Peter answered him, LORD, to whom shall we go? thou hast the words of eternal life.

And we believe and are sure that thou art that Christ, the Son of the living God.

John 6:67-69

And there was in their synagogue a man with an unclean spirit; and he cried out,

Saying, Let us alone; what have we to do with thee, thou Jesus of Nazareth? Art thou come to destroy us? I know thee who thou art, the Holy One of God.

Mark 1:23, 24

*   *   *   *

Thus saith the LORD, the Redeemer of Israel, and his Holy One, to him whom man despiseth, to him whom the nation abhorreth, to a servant of rulers, Kings shall see and arise, princes also shall worship, because of the LORD that is faithful, and the Holy One of Israel, and he shall choose thee.

Isaiah 49:7

Yea, every pot in Jerusalem and in Judah shall be holiness unto the LORD of hosts: and all they that sacrifice shall come and take of them, and seethe therein: in that day there shall be no more the Cananite in the house of the LORD of hosts.

Zechariah 14:21

And to the angel of the church in Philadelphia write; These things saith he that is holy, he that is true, he that hath the key of David, he that openeth, and no man shutteth; and shutteth, and no man openeth.

Revelation 3:7

*   *   *   *

For thus saith the high and lofty One that inhabiteth eternity, whose name is Holy; I dwell in the high and holy place, with him also that is of a contrite and humble spirit, to revive the spirit of the humble, and to revive the heart of the contrite ones.

Isaiah 57:15

But ye have an unction from the Holy One, and ye know all things.

1 John 2:20

*   *   *   *

Sanctify the LORD of hosts himself; and let him be your fear, and let him be your dread.

Isaiah 8:13

And in the synagogue there was a man, which had a spirit of an unclean devil, and cried out with a loud voice,

Saying, Let us alone; what have we to do with thee, thou Jesus of Nazareth? Art thou come to destroy us? I know thee who thou art; the Holy One of God.

Luke 4:33, 34

There is none holy as the LORD: for there is none beside thee: neither is there any rock like our God.

1 Samuel 2:2

But ye denied the Holy One and the Just, and desired a murderer to be granted unto you.

Acts 3:14

*   *   *   *

And it shall be in that day, that living waters shall go out from Jerusalem; half of them toward the former sea, and half of them toword the hinder sea: in summer and in winter shall it be.

And the LORD shall be king over all the earth: in that day shall there be one LORD, and his name one.

In that day shall there be upon the bells of the horses, HOLINESS UNTO THE LORD; and the pots in the LORD's house shall be like the bowls before the altar.

Zechariah 14:8, 9, 20

Yea, every pot in Jerusalem and in Judah shall be holiness unto the LORD of hosts: and all they that sacrifice shall come and take of them, and seethe therein: and in that day there shall be no more the Canaanite in the house of the LORD of hosts.

Zechariah 14:21

I will not execute the fierceness of mine anger, I will not return to destroy Ephraim: for I am God, and not man; the Holy One in the midst of thee: and I will not enter into the city.

Hosea 11:9

John did baptize in the wilderness, and preach the baptism of repentance for the remission of sins.

Mark 1:4

HIS EXAMPLE

*(Jesus, the Messiah, gave us an example to follow,
through His words and His actions.)*

Take my yoke upon you, and learn of me; for I am meek and lowly in heart: and ye shall find rest unto your souls.

Matthew 11:29

Even as the Son of man came not to be ministered unto, but to minister, and to give his life a ransom for many.

Matthew 20:28

But so shall it not be among you: but whosoever will be great among you, shall be your minister.

Mark 10:43

Ye call me Master and LORD: and ye say well; for so I am.
A new commandment I give unto you, That ye love one another; as I have loved you, that ye also love one another.

John 13:13, 34

As thou hast sent me into the world, even so have I also sent them into the world.

John 17:18

Let every one of us please his neighbour for his good to edification.

Romans 15:2

And walk in love, as Christ also hath loved us, and hath given himself for us an offering and a sacrifice to God for a sweet-smelling savour.

Ephesians 5:2

Let this mind be in you, which was also in Christ Jesus:
Who, being in the form of God, thought it not robbery to be equal with God: But made himself of no reputation, and took upon him the form of a servant, and was made in the likeness of men:
And being found in fashion as a man, he humbled himself, and became obedient unto death, even the death of the cross.

Philippians 2:5-8

Looking unto Jesus the author and finisher of our faith, who for the joy that was set before him endured the cross, despising the shame, and is set down at the right hand of the throne of God.

Hebrews 12:2

He that saith, I know him, and keepeth not his commandments, is a liar, and the truth is not in him.

But whoso keepeth his word, in him verily is the love of God perfected: hereby know we that we are in him.

He that saith he abideth in him ought himself also so to walk, even as he walked.

1 John 2:4-6

HIS HUMANITY

Therefore the Lord himself shall give you a sign; Behold, a virgin shall conceive, and bear a son, and shall call his name Immanuel.

Isaiah 7:14

And, behold, thou shalt conceive in thy womb, and bring forth a son, and shalt call his name JESUS.

Luke 1:31

And the Word was made flesh, and dwelt among us, (and we beheld his glory, the glory as of the only begotten of the Father,) full of grace and truth.

John 1:14

* * * *

So the spirit took me up, and brought me into the inner court; and, behold, the glory of the Lord filled the house.

And I heard him speaking unto me out of the house; and the man stood by me.

And he said unto me, Son of man, the place of my throne, and the place of the soles of my feet, where I will dwell in the midst of the children of Israel for ever, and my holy name, shall the house of Israel no more defile, neither they, nor their kings, by their whoredom, nor by the carcases of their kings in their high places.

Ezekiel 43:5-7

The Jews answered him, saying, For a good work we stone thee not; but for blasphemy; and because that thou, being a man, makest thyself God.

John 10:33

But we see Jesus, who was made a little lower than the angels for the suffering of death, crowned with glory and honour; that he by the grace of God should taste death for every man.

Hebrews 2:9

For verily he took not on him the nature of angels; but he took on him the seed of Abraham.

Wherefore in all things it behoved him to be made like unto his brethren, that he might be a merciful and faithful high priest in things pertaining to God, to make reconciliation for the sins of the people.

For in that he himself hath suffered being tempted, he is able to succour them that are tempted.

Hebrews 2:16-18

* * * *

And I will put enmity between thee and the woman, and between thy seed and her seed; it shall bruise thy head, and thou shalt bruise his heel.

Genesis 3:15

And Joseph also went up from Galilee. . .

To be taxed with Mary his espoused wife, being great with child.

And so it was, that, while they were there, the days were accomplished that she should be delivered.

Luke 2:4-6

Hereby know ye the Spirit of God: Every spirit that confesseth that Jesus Christ is come in the flesh is of God.

1 John 4:2

And without controversy great is the mystery of godliness: God was manifest in the flesh, justified in the Spirit, seen of angels, preached unto the Gentiles, believed on in the world, received up into glory.

1 Timothy 3:16

OTHER INDICATIONS
OF THE MESSIAH'S HUMANITY

1. His physical growth (Luke 2:40, 52).
2. He spoke of Himself as a man (John 8:40).
3. Others spoke of Him as a man (Acts 2:22).
4. He got hungry (Matthew 4:2; Luke 4:2).
5. He became thirsty (John 19:28).
6. He grew weary and physically tired (John 4:6).
7. He needed sleep (Matthew 8:24; Luke 8:23).
8. He was homeless and economically impoverished (Luke 9:58).
9. He wept (John 11:35).
10. He expressed love and compassion (Matthew 9:36).
11. He became angry (Matthew 21:13).
12. He expressed sorrow (Matthew 26:37).
13. He was troubled in His soul (John 12:27).

HIS CLAIMS TO BE GOD
(and His Equality with God)

The voice of him that crieth in the wilderness, Prepare ye the way of the LORD, make straight in the desert a highway for our God.

Isaiah 40:3

For this is he that was spoken of by the prophet Esaias, saying, The voice of one crying in the wilderness, Prepare ye the way of the LORD, make his paths straight.

Matthew 3:3

* * * *

Lift up your heads, O ye gates; and be ye lift up, ye everlasting doors; and the King of glory shall come in.

Who is this King of glory? The LORD of hosts, he is the King of glory. Selah.

Psalm 24:7, 10

Which none of the princes of this world knew: for had they known it, they would not have crucified the LORD of glory.

1 Corinthians 2:8

My brethren, have not the faith of our LORD Jesus Christ, the LORD of glory, with respect of persons.

James 2:1

Behold, the days come, saith the LORD, that I will raise unto David a righteous Branch, and a King shall reign and prosper, and shall execute judgment and justice in the earth.

In his days Judah shall be saved, and Israel shall dwell safely: and this is his name whereby he shall be called, THE LORD OUR RIGHTEOUSNESS.

Jeremiah 23:5, 6

But of him are ye in Christ Jesus, who of God is made unto us wisdom, and righteousness, and sanctification, and redemption.

1 Corinthians 1:30

* * * *

I will declare the decree: the LORD hath said unto me, Thou art my Son; this day have I begotten thee.

Psalm 2:7

And was there until the death of Herod: that it might be fulfilled which was spoken of the LORD by the prophet, saying, Out of Egypt have I called my son.

Matthew 2:15

And lo a voice from heaven saying, This is my beloved Son, in whom I am well pleased.

Matthew 3:17

And, behold, they cried out, saying, What have we to do with thee, Jesus, thou Son of God? art thou come hither to torment us before the time?

Matthew 8:29

Then they that were in the ship came and worshipped him, saying, Of a truth thou art the Son of God.

Matthew 14:33

While he yet spake, behold, a bright cloud overshadowed them: and behold a voice out of the cloud, which said, This is my beloved Son, in whom I am well pleased; hear ye him.

Matthew 17:5

And straightway he preached Christ in the synagogues, that he is the Son of God.

Acts 9:20

Of how much sorer punishment, suppose ye, shall he be thought worthy, who hath trodden under foot the Son of God, and hath counted the blood of the covenant, wherewith he was sanctified, an unholy thing, and hath done despite unto the Spirit of grace?

Hebrews 10:29

Whosoever shall confess that Jesus is the Son of God, God dwelleth in him, and he in God.

1 John 4:15

HIS CLAIMS TO BE
THE MESSIAH

Know therefore and understand, that from the going forth of the commandment to restore and to build Jerusalem unto the Messiah the Prince shall be seven weeks, and threescore and two weeks: the street shall be built again, and the wall, even in troublous times.

And after threescore and two weeks shall Messiah be cut off, but not for himself: and the people of the prince that shall come shall destroy the city and the sanctuary; and the end thereof shall be with a flood, and unto the end of the war desolations are determined.

Daniel 9:25, 26

He saith unto them, But whom say ye that I am?

And Simon Peter answered and said, Thou art the Christ, the Son of the living God.

Matthew 16:15, 16

And said unto him, Art thou he that should come, or do we look for another?

Jesus answered and said unto them, Go and shew John again those things which ye do hear and see:

The blind receive their sight, and the lame walk, the lepers are cleansed, and the deaf hear, the dead are raised up, and the poor have the gospel preached to them.

And blessed is he, whosoever shall not be offended in me.

Matthew 11:3-6

But Jesus held his peace. And the high priest answered and said unto him, I adjure thee by the living God, that thou tell us whether thou be the Christ, the Son of God.

Jesus saith unto him, Thou hast said: nevertheless I say unto you, Hereafter shall ye see the Son of man sitting on the right hand of power, and coming in the clouds of heaven.

Then the high priest rent his clothes, saying, He hath spoken blasphemy; what further need have we of witnesses? behold, now ye have heard his blasphemy.

Matthew 26:63-65

Search the scriptures; for in them ye think ye have eternal life: and they are they which testify of me.

John 5:39

The woman saith unto him, I know that Messias cometh, which is called Christ: when he is come, he will tell us all things. Jesus saith unto her, I that speak unto thee am he.

John 4:25, 26

As Messiah, Jesus claimed:

1. Equality with the Father

That all men should honour the Son, even as they honour the Father. He that honoureth not the Son honoreth not the Father which hath sent him.

John 5:23

Jesus saith unto him, Have I been so long time with you, and yet hast thou not known me, Philip? he that hath seen me hath seen the Father; and how sayest thou then, Shew us the Father?

Believest thou not that I am in the Father, and the Father in me? the words that I speak unto you I speak not of myself: but the Father that dwelleth in me, he doeth the works.

He that loveth me not keepeth not my sayings: and the word which ye hear is not mine, but the Father's which sent me.

John 14:9, 10, 24

And he that seeth me seeth him that sent me.

John 12:45

But Saul increased the more in strength, and confounded the Jews which dwelt at Damascus, proving that this is very Christ.

Acts 9:22

Whosoever believeth that Jesus is the Christ is born of God: and every one that loveth him that begat loveth him also that is begotten of him.

1 John 5:1

2. A unique relationship with the Father

All things are delivered unto me of my Father: and no man knoweth the Son, but the Father; neither knoweth any man the Father, save the Son, and he to whomsoever the Son will reveal him.

Matthew 11:27

But Jesus answered them, My Father worketh hitherto, and I work.

John 5:17

If ye had known me, ye should have known my Father also: and from henceforth ye know him, and have seen him.

Philip saith unto him, LORD, shew us the Father, and it sufficeth us.

Jesus saith unto him, Have I been so long time with you, and yet

200

hast thou not known me, Philip? he that hath seen me hath seen the Father; and how sayest thou then, Shew us the Father?

Believest thou not that I am in the Father, and the Father in me? the words that I speak unto you I speak not of myself: but the Father that dwelleth in me, he doeth the works.

John 14:7-10

I and my Father are one.

Say ye of him, whom the Father hath sanctified, and sent into the world, Thou blasphemest; because I said, I am the Son of God?

John 10:30, 36

3. To be able to satisfy man's deepest needs

And Jesus said unto them, I am the bread of life: he that cometh to me shall never hunger; and he that believeth on me shall never thirst.

John 6:35

But whosoever drinketh of the water that I shall give him shall never thirst; but the water that I shall give him shall be in him a well of water springing up into everlasting life.

John 4:14

4. To provide eternal life and safety

My sheep hear my voice, and I know them, and they follow me:

And I give unto them eternal life; and they shall never perish, neither shall any man pluck them out of my hand.

My Father, which gave them me, is greater than all; and no man is able to pluck them out of my Father's hand.

John 10:27-29

All that the Father giveth me shall come to me; and him that cometh to me I will in no wise cast out.

For I came down from heaven, not to do mine own will, but the will of him that sent me.

And this is the Father's will which hath sent me, that of all which he hath given me I should lose nothing, but should raise it up again at the last day.

And this is the will of him that sent me, that every one which seeth the Son, and believeth on him, may have everlasting life: and I will raise him up at the last day.

John 6:37-40

JESUS' STATEMENTS
CLAIMING TO BE GOD

I and my Father are one.

John 10:30

The Jews answered him, We have a law, and by our law he ought to die, because he made himself the Son of God.

John 19:7

But Jesus held his peace. And the high priest answered and said unto him, I adjure thee by the living God, that thou tell us whether thou be the Christ, the Son of God.

Jesus saith unto him, Thou hast said: nevertheless I say unto you, Hereafter shall ye see the Son of man sitting on the right hand of power, and coming in the clouds of heaven.

Matthew 26:63-64

Therefore the Jews sought the more to kill him, because he not only had broken the sabbath, but said also that God was his Father, making himself equal with God.

John 5:18

Which of you convinceth me of sin? And if I say the truth, why do ye not believe me?

John 8:46

For had ye believed Moses, ye would have believed me: for he wrote of me.

But if ye believe not his writings, how shall ye believe my words?

John 5:46, 47

Then he said unto them, O fools, and slow of heart to believe all that the prophets have spoken:

Ought not Christ to have suffered these things, and to enter into his glory?

And beginning at Moses and all the prophets, he expounded unto them in all the scriptures the things concerning himself.

Luke 24:25-27

And he said unto them, These are the words which I spake unto you, while I was yet with you, that all things must be fulfilled, which were written in the law of Moses, and in the prophets, and in the psalms, concerning me.

Then opened he their understanding, that they might understand the scriptures,

And said unto them, Thus it is written, and thus it behoved Christ to suffer, and to rise from the dead the third day:

And that repentance and remission of sins should be preached in his name among all nations, beginning at Jerusalem.

Luke 24:44-47

HIS JUDGMENT

For the LORD is our judge, the LORD is our lawgiver, the LORD is our king; he will save us.

Isaiah 33:22

I can of mine own self do nothing: as I hear, I judge: and my judgment is just; because I seek not mine own will, but the will of the Father which hath sent me.

John 5:30

I charge thee therefore before God, and the LORD Jesus Christ, who shall judge the quick and the dead at his appearing and his kingdom.

2 Timothy 4:1

But ye are come unto mount Sion, and unto the city of the living God, the heavenly Jerusalem, and to an innumerable company of angels,

To the general assembly and church of the firstborn, which are written in heaven, and to God the Judge of all, and to the spirits of just men made perfect,

And to Jesus the mediator of the new covenant, and to the blood of sprinkling, that speaketh better things than that of Abel.

Hebrews 12:22-24

He shall judge thy people with righteousness, and thy poor with judgment.

The mountains shall bring peace to the people, and the little hills, by righteousness.

He shall judge the poor of the people, he shall save the children of the needy, and shall break in pieces the oppressor.

Psalm 72:2-4

Behold my servant, whom I uphold; mine elect, in whom my soul delighteth; I have put my spirit upon him: he shall bring forth judgment to the Gentiles.

He shall not fail nor be discouraged, till he have set judgment in the earth: and the isles shall wait for his law.

Isaiah 42:1, 4

And as he spake, a certain Pharisee besought him to dine with him: and he went in, and sat down to meat.

And when the Pharisee saw it, he marvelled that he had

not first washed before dinner.

And the LORD said unto him, Now do ye Pharisees make clean the outside of the cup and the platter; but your inward part is full of ravening and wickedness.

Luke 11:37-39

* * * *

But with righteousness shall he judge the poor, and reprove with equity for the meek of the earth: and he shall smite the earth with the rod of his mouth, and with the breath of his lips shall he slay the wicked.

Isaiah 11:4

And I saw a great white throne, and him that sat on it, from whose face the earth and the heaven fled away; and there was found no place for them.

And I saw the dead, small and great, stand before God; and the books were opened: and another book was opened, which is the book of life: and the dead were judged out of those things which were written in the books, according to their works.

And the sea gave up the dead which were in it; and death and hell delivered up the dead which were in them: and they were judged every man according to their works.

And death and hell were cast into the lake of fire. This is the second death.

And whosoever was not found written in the book of life was cast into the lake of fire.

Revelation 20:11-15

Then shall he say also unto them on the left hand, Depart from me, ye cursed, into everlasting fire, prepared for the devil and his angels.

Matthew 25:41

For we must all appear before the judgment seat of Christ; that every one may receive the things done in his body, according to that he hath done, whether it be good or bad.

2 Corinthians 5:10

He shall judge thy people with righteousness, and thy poor with judgment.

Psalm 72:2

He shall judge among the heathen, he shall fill the places with the dead bodies; he shall wound the heads over many countries.

Psalm 110:6

And he commanded us to preach unto the people, and to testify that it is he which was ordained of God to be the Judge of quick and dead.

Acts 10:42

And the times of this ignorance God winked at; but now commandeth all men every where to repent:

Because he hath appointed a day, in the which he will judge the world in righteousness by that man whom he hath ordained; whereof he hath given assurance unto all men, in that he hath raised him from the dead.

Acts 17:30, 31

In the day when God shall judge the secrets of men by Jesus Christ according to my gospel.

Romans 2:16

But why dost thou judge thy brother? Or why dost thou set at nought thy brother? For we shall all stand before the judgment seat of Christ.

Romans 14:10

HIS KINGSHIP

Ask of me, and I shall give thee the heathen for thine inheritance, and the uttermost parts of the earth for thy possession.

Psalm 2:8

And he shall rule them with a rod of iron; as the vessels of a potter shall they be broken to shivers: even as I received of my Father.

Revelation 2:27

* * * *

And the LORD shall be king over all the earth: in that day shall there be one LORD, and his name one.

Zechariah 14:9

The LORD said unto my LORD, Sit thou at my right hand, until I make thine enemies thy footstool.

The lord shall send the rod of thy strength out of Zion: rule thou in the midst of thine enemies.

Thy people shall be willing in the day of thy power, in the beauties of holiness from the womb of the morning: thou hast the dew of thy youth.

Psalm 110:1-3

For David is not ascended into the heavens: but he saith himself, The LORD said unto my LORD, Sit thou on my right hand,

Until I make thy foes thy footstool.

Acts 2:34-35

For he must reign, till he hath put all enemies under his feet.

1 Corinthians 15:25

And the seventh angel sounded; and there were great voices in heaven, saying, The kingdoms of this world are become the kingdoms of our LORD, and of his Christ; and he shall reign for ever and ever.

Revelation 11:15

* * * *

And it shall come to pass, that every one that is left of all the nations which came against Jerusalem shall even go up from year to year to worship the King, the LORD of hosts, and to keep the feast of tabernacles.

Zechariah 14:16

Jesus answered, My kingdom is not of this world: if my kingdom were of this world, then would my servants fight, that I should not be delivered to the Jews: but now is my kingdom not from hence.

Pilate therefore said unto him, Art thou a king then? Jesus answered, Thou sayest that I am a king. To this end was I born, and for this cause came I into the world, that I should bear witness unto the truth. Every one that is of the truth heareth my voice.

John 18:36, 37

*   *   *   *

For unto us a child is born, unto us a son is given: and the government shall be upon his shoulder: and his name shall be called Wonderful, Counsellor, The mighty God, The everlasting Father, The Prince of Peace.

Isaiah 9:6

For he is our peace, who hath made both one, and hath broken down the middle wall of partition between us:

Having abolished in his flesh the enmity, even the law of commandments contained in ordinances; for to make in himself of twain one new man, so making peace;

And that he might reconcile both unto God in one body by the cross, having slain the enmity thereby:

And came and preached peace to you which were afar off, and to them that were nigh.

For through him we both have access by one Spirit unto the Father.

Ephesians 2:14-18

And in the days of these kings shall the God of heaven set up a kingdom, which shall never be destroyed: and the kingdom shall not be left to other people, but it shall break in pieces and consume all these kingdoms, and it shall stand for ever.

Daniel 2:44

And at the end of the days I Nebuchadnezzar lifted up mine eyes unto heaven, and mine understanding returned unto me, and I blessed the most High, and I praised and honoured him that liveth for ever, whose dominion is an everlasting dominion, and his kingdom is from generation to generation.

Daniel 4:34

I saw in the night visions, and, behold, one like the Son of man came with the clouds of heaven, and came to the Ancient of days, and they brought him near before him.

And there was given him dominion, and glory, and a kingdom, that all people, nations, and languages, should serve him: his dominion is an everlasting dominion, which shall not pass away, and his kingdom that which shall not be destroyed.

And the kingdom and dominion, and the greatness of the kingdom under the whole heaven, shall be given to the people of the saints of the most High, whose kingdom is an everlasting kingdom, and all dominions shall serve and obey him.

Daniel 7:13, 14, 27

And he shall reign over the house of Jacob for ever; and of his kingdom there shall be no end.

Luke 1:33

Wherefore we receiving a kingdom which cannot be moved, let us have grace, whereby we may serve God acceptably with reverence and godly fear.

Hebrews 12:28

*   *   *   *

Moreover I will appoint a place for my people Israel, and will plant them, that they may dwell in a place of their own, and move no more; neither shall the children of wickedness afflict them any more, as beforetime,

And as since the time that I commanded judges to be over my people Israel, and have caused thee to rest from all thine enemies. Also the LORD telleth thee that he will make thee an house.

And when thy days are fulfilled, and thou shalt sleep with

thy fathers, I will set up thy seed after thee, which shall proceed out of thy bowels, and I will establish his kingdom.

He shall build an house for my name, and I will establish the throne of his kingdom for ever.

I will be his father, and he shall be my son. If he commit iniquity, I will chasten him with the rod of men, and with the stripes of the children of men:

But my mercy shall not depart away from him, as I took it from Saul, whom I put away before thee.

And thine house and thy kingdom shall be established for ever before thee: thy throne shall be established for ever.

2 Samuel 7:10-16

Of the increase of his government and peace there shall be no end, upon the throne of David, and upon his kingdom, to order it, and to establish it with judgment and with justice from henceforth even for ever. The zeal of the LORD of hosts will perform this.

Isaiah 9:7

Behold, the days come, saith the LORD, that I will raise unto David a righteous Branch, and a King shall reign and prosper, and shall execute judgment and justice in the earth.

Jeremiah 23:5

And, behold, thou shalt conceive in thy womb, and bring forth a son, and shalt call his name JESUS.

He shall be great, and shall be called the Son of the Highest: and the LORD God shall give unto him the throne of his father David.

Luke 1:31, 32

And out of his mouth goeth a sharp sword, that with it he should smite the nations: and he shall rule them with a rod of iron: and he treadeth the winepress of the fierceness and wrath of Almighty God.

Revelation 19:15

These shall make war with the Lamb, and the Lamb shall overcome them: for he is LORD of LORDs, and King of kings: and they that are with him are called, and chosen, and faithful.

Revelation 17:14

* * * *

Yet have I set my king upon my holy hill of Zion.

I will declare the decree: the LORD hath said unto me, Thou art my Son; this day have I begotten thee.

Ask of me, and I shall give thee the heathen for thine inheritance, and the uttermost parts of the earth for thy possession.

Thou shalt break them with a rod of iron; thou shalt dash them in pieces like a potter's vessel.

Psalm 2:6-9

He shall have dominion also from sea to sea, and from the river unto the ends of the earth.

They that dwell in the wilderness shall bow before him; and his enemies shall lick the dust.

The kings of Tarshish and of the isles shall bring presents: the kings of Sheba and Seba shall offer gifts.

Yea, all kings shall fall down before him: all nations shall serve him.

Psalms 72:8-11

And there shall come forth a rod out of the stem of Jesse; and a Branch shall grow out of his roots:

And the spirit of the LORD shall rest upon him, the spirit of wisdom and understanding, the spirit of counsel and might, the spirit of knowledge and of the fear of the LORD;

And shall make him of quick understanding in the fear of the LORD: and he shall not judge after the sight of his eyes, neither reprove after the hearing of his ears:

But with the righteousness shall he judge the poor, and reprove with equity for the meek of the earth: and he shall smite the earth with the breath of his lips shall he slay the wicked.

And righteousness shall be the girdle of his loins, and faithfulness the girdle of his reins.

The wolf also shall dwell with the lamb, and the leopard shall lie down with the kid; and the calf and the young lion and the fatling together; and a little child shall lead them.

And the cow and the bear shall feed; their young ones shall lie down together: and the lion shall eat straw like the ox.

And the sucking child shall play on the hole of the asp, and the weaned child shall put his hand on the cockatrice' den.

They shall not hurt nor destroy in all my holy mountain:

for the earth shall be full of the knowledge of the LORD, as the waters cover the sea.

Isaiah 11:1-9

Rejoice greatly, O daughter of Zion; shout, O daughter of Jerusalem: behold, thy King cometh unto thee: he is just, and having salvation; lowly, and riding upon an ass, and upon a colt the foal of an ass.

Zechariah 9:9

Tell ye the daughter of Sion, Behold, thy King cometh unto thee, meek, and sitting upon an ass, and a colt the foal of an ass.

Matthew 21:5

And I saw heaven opened, and behold a white horse; and he that sat upon him was called Faithful and True, and in righteousness he doth judge and make war.

His eyes were as a flame of fire, and on his head were many crowns; and he had a name written, that no man knew, but he himself.

And he was clothed with a vesture dipped in blood: and his name is called The Word of God.

And the armies which were in heaven followed him upon white horses, clothed in fine linen, white and clean.

And out of his mouth goeth a sharp sword, that with it he should smite the nations: and he shall rule them with a rod of iron: and he treadeth the winepress of the fierceness and wrath of Almighty God.

And he hath on his vesture and on his thigh a name written, KING OF KINGS, AND LORD OF LORDS.

Revelation 19:11-16

And set up over his head his accusation written, THIS IS JESUS THE KING OF THE JEWS.

Matthew 27:37

Then Pilate entered into the judgment hall again, and called Jesus, and said unto him, Art thou the King of the Jews?

Jesus answered him, Sayest thou this thing of thyself, or did others tell it thee of me?

Pilate answered him, Am I a Jew? Thine own nation and the chief priests have delivered thee unto me: what hast thou done?

Jesus answered, My kingdom is not of this world: if my kingdom were of this world, then would my servants fight, that I should not be delivered to the Jews: but now is my kingdom not from hence.

John 18:33-36

Him hath God exalted with his right hand to be a Prince and a Saviour, for to give repentance to Israel, and forgiveness of sins.

And we are his witnesses of these things; and so is also the Holy Ghost, whom God hath given to them that obey him.

Acts 5:31, 32

Which in his times he shall shew, who is the blessed and only Potentate, the King of kings, and LORD of lords.

1 Timothy 6:15

And from Jesus Christ, who is the faithful witness, and the first begotten of the dead, and the prince of the kings of the earth. Unto him that loved us, and washed us from our sins in his own blood.

Revelation 1:5

Nathanael answered and saith unto him, Rabbi, thou art the Son of God; thou art the King of Israel.

John 1:49

JESUS, KING OF KINGS
& LORD OF LORDS

The LORD said unto my LORD, Sit thou at my right hand, until I make thine enemies thy footstool.

Psalm 110:1

In his days Judah shall be saved, and Israel shall dwell safely: and this is his name whereby he shall be called, THE LORD OUR RIGHTEOUSNESS.

Jeremiah 23:6

The adversaries of the LORD shall be broken to pieces; out of heaven shall he thunder upon them: the LORD shall judge the ends of the earth; and he shall give strength unto his king, and exalt the horn of his anointed.

1 Samuel 2:10

For I know that my redeemer liveth, and that he shall stand at the latter day upon the earth.

Job 19:25

For unto you is born this day in the city of David a Saviour, which is Christ the LORD.

Luke 2:11

And he said unto them, How say they that Christ is David's son?

And David himself saith in the book of Psalms, The LORD said unto my LORD, Sit thou on my right hand,

Till I make thine enemies thy footstool.

David therefore calleth him LORD, how is he then his son?

Luke 20:41-44

While the Pharisees were gathered together, Jesus asked them,

Saying, What think ye of Christ? Whose son is he? They say unto him, The son of David.

He saith unto them, How then doth David in spirit call him LORD, saying,

The LORD said unto my LORD, Sit thou on my right hand, till I make thine enemies thy footstool?

Matthew 22:41-44

* * * *

And I Daniel alone saw the vision: for the men that were with me saw not the vision; but a great quaking fell upon them, so that they fled to hide themselves.

Daniel 10:7

These shall make war with the Lamb, and the Lamb shall overcome them: for he is LORD of lords, and King of kings: and they that are with him are called, and chosen, and faithful.

Revelation 17:14

And from Jesus Christ, who is the faithful witness, and the first begotten of the dead, and the prince of the kings of the earth. Unto him that loved us, and washed us from our sins in his own blood.

Revelation 1:5

And the seventh angel sounded; and there were great voices in heaven, saying, The kingdoms of this world are become the kingdoms of our LORD, and of his Christ; and he shall reign for ever and ever.

Revelation 11:15

And I heard a loud voice saying in heaven, Now is come salvation, and strength, and the kingdom of our God, and the power of his Christ: for the accuser of our brethren is cast down, which accused them before our God day and night.

Revelation 12:10

And I looked, and behold a white cloud, and upon the cloud one sat like unto the Son of man, having on his head a golden crown, and in his hand a sharp sickle.

Revelation 14:14

And I saw heaven opened, and behold a white horse; and he that sat upon him was called Faithful and True, and in righteousness he doth judge and make war,

His eyes were as a flame of fire, and on his head were many crowns; and he had a name written, that no man knew, but he himself.

And he was clothed with a vesture dipped in blood: and his name is called The Word of God.

And the armies which were in heaven followed him upon white horses, clothed in fine linen, white and clean.

And out of his mouth goeth a sharp sword, that with it he

should smite the nations: and he shall rule them with a rod of iron: and he treadeth the winepress of the fierceness and wrath of Almighty God.

And he hath on his vesture and on his thigh a name written, KING OF KINGS, AND LORD OF LORDS.

Revelation 19:11-16

* * * *

Tell ye, and bring them near: yea, let them take counsel together: who hath declared this from ancient time? who hath told it from that time? have not I the LORD? And there is no God else beside me; a just God and a Saviour; there is none beside me.

Look unto me, and be ye saved, all the ends of the earth: for I am God, and there is none else.

I have sworn by myself, the word is gone out of my mouth in righteousness, and shall not return, That unto me every knee shall bow, and every tongue shall swear.

Isaiah 45:21-23

That at the name of Jesus every knee should bow, of things in heaven, and things in earth, and things under the earth;

And that every tongue should confess that Jesus Christ is LORD, to the glory of God the Father.

Philippians 2:10, 11

THE LAMB OF GOD

Your lamb shall be without blemish, a male of the first year: ye shall take it out from the sheep, or from the goats.

Exodus 12:5

Purge out therefore the old leaven, that ye may be a new lump, as ye are unleavened. For even Christ our passover is sacrificed for us.

1 Corinthians 5:7

But with the precious blood of Christ, as of a lamb without blemish and without spot.

1 Peter 1:19

And I saw no temple therein: for the LORD Almighty and the Lamb are the temple of it.

Revelation 21:22

And I saw when the Lamb opened one of the seals, and I heard, as it were the noise of the thunder, one of the four beasts saying, Come and see.

Revelation 6:1

*   *   *   *

And if he bring a lamb for a sin offering, he shall bring it a female without blemish.

And he shall lay his hand upon the head of the sin offering, and slay if for a sin offering in the place where they kill the burnt offering.

And the priest shall take of the blood of the sin offering with his finger, and put it upon the horns of the altar of burnt offering, and shall pour out all the blood thereof at the bottom of the altar:

And he shall take away all the fat thereof, as the fat of a lamb is taken away from the sacrifice of the peace offerings; and the priest shall burn them upon the altar, according to the offerings made by fire unto the LORD: and the priest shall make an atonement for his sin that he hath committed, and it shall be forgiven him.

Leviticus 4:32-35

He was oppressed, and he was afflicted, yet he opened not his mouth: he is brought as a lamb to the slaughter, and as

217

a sheep before her shearers is dumb, so he openeth not his mouth.

Isaiah 53:7

And I beheld, and, lo, in the midst of the throne and of the four beasts, and in the midst of the elders, stood a Lamb as it had been slain, having seven horns and seven eyes, which are the seven Spirits of God sent forth into all the earth.

And when he had taken the book, the four beasts and four and twenty elders fell down before the Lamb, having every one of them harps, and golden vials full of odours, which are the prayers of saints.

Revelation 5:6, 8

Saying with a loud voice, Worthy is the Lamb that was slain to receive power, and riches, and wisdom, and strength, and honour, and glory, and blessing.

And every creature which is in heaven, and on the earth, and under the earth, and such as are in the sea, and all that are in them, heard I saying, Blessing, and honour, and glory, and power, be unto him that sitteth upon the throne, and unto the Lamb for ever and ever.

Revelation 5:12, 13

The next day John seeth Jesus coming unto him, and saith, Behold the Lamb of God, which taketh away the sin of the world.

John 1:29

For I delivered unto you first of all that which I also received, how that Christ died for our sins according to the scriptures.

1 Corinthians 15:3

And they sing the song of Moses the servant of God, and the song of the Lamb, saying, Great and marvellous are thy works, LORD God Almighty; just and true are thy ways, thou King of saints.

Revelation 15:3

And there came unto me one of the seven angels which had the seven vials full of the seven last plagues, and talked with me, saying, Come hither, I will shew thee the bride, the Lamb's wife.

And the wall of the city had twelve foundations, and in them the names of the twelve apostles of the Lamb.

And I saw no temple therein: for the LORD God Almighty and the Lamb are the temple of it.

And the city had no need of the sun, neither of the moon, to shine in it: for the glory of God did lighten it, and the Lamb is the light thereof.

And there shall in no wise enter into it any thing that defileth, neither whatsoever worketh abomination, or maketh a lie: but they which are written in the Lamb's book of life.

Revelation 21:9, 14, 22, 23, 27

* * * *

And the priest shall make an atonement for all the congregation of the children of Israel, and it shall be forgiven them; for it is ignorance: and they shall bring their offering, a sacrifice made by fire unto the LORD, and their sin offering before the LORD, for their ignorance:

And it shall be forgiven all the congregation of the children of Israel, and the stranger that sojourneth among them; seeing all the people were in ignorance.

Numbers 15:25, 26

And every priest standeth daily ministering and offering oftentimes the same sacrifices, which can never take away sins.

Hebrews 10:11

Which was a figure for the time then present, in which were offered both gifts and sacrifices, that could not make him that did the service perfect, as pertaining to the conscience.

Hebrews 9:9

For the law having a shadow of good things to come, and not the very image of the things, can never with those sacrifices which they offered year by year continually make the comers thereunto perfect.

For then would they not have ceased to be offered? because that the worshippers once purged should have had no more conscience of sins.

Hebrews 10:1, 2

But now hath he obtained a more excellent ministry, by

how much also he is the mediator of a better covenant, which was established upon better promises.

For if that first covenant had been faultless, then should no place have been sought for the second.

For finding fault with them, he saith, Behold, the days come, saith the LORD, when I will make a new covenant with the house of Israel and with the house of Judah:

Not according to the covenant that I made with their fathers in the day when I took them by the hand to lead them out of the land of Egypt; because they continued not in my covenant, and I regarded them not, saith the LORD.

For this is the covenant that I will make with the house of Israel after those days, saith the LORD; I will put my laws into their mind, and write them in their hearts: and I will be to them a God, and they shall be to me a people:

And they shall not teach every man his neighbour, and every man his brother, saying, Know the LORD: for all shall know me, from the least to the greatest.

For I will be merciful to their unrighteousness, and their sins and their iniquities will I remember no more.

In that he saith, A new covenant, he hath made the first old. Now that which decayeth and waxeth old is ready to vanish away.

Hebrews 8:6-13

Likewise also the cup after supper, saying, This cup is the new testament in my blood, which is shed for you.

Luke 22:20

HIS INTERCESSION

Therefore will I divide him a portion with the great, and he shall divide the spoil with the strong; because he hath poured our his soul unto death: and he was numbered with the transgressors; and he bare the sin of many, and made intercession for the transgressors.

Isaiah 53:12

Then said Jesus, Father, forgive them; for they know not what they do. And they parted his raiment, and cast lots.

Luke 23:34

For Christ is not entered into the holy places made with hands, which are the figures of the true; but into heaven itself, now to appear in the presence of God for us.

Hebrews 9:24

My little children, these things write I unto you, that ye sin not. And if any man sin, we have an advocate with the Father, Jesus Christ the righteous.

1 John 2:1

* * * *

And, behold, I am with thee, and will keep thee in all places whither thou goest, and will bring thee again into this land; for I will not leave thee, until I have done that which I have spoken to thee of.

Genesis 28:15

Wherefore he is able also to save them to the uttermost that come unto God by him, seeing he ever liveth to make intercession for them.

Hebrews 7:25

I pray for them: I pray not for the world, but for them which thou hast given me; for they are thine.

John 17:9

But I have prayed for thee, that thy faith fail not: and when thou art converted, strengthen thy brethren.

Luke 22:32

THE GOD OF ISRAEL

Jehovah, the King of Glory.

Lift up your heads, O ye gates; and be ye lift up, ye everlasting doors; and the King of glory shall come in.

Who is this King of glory? The LORD of hosts, he is the King of glory. Selah.

Psalm 24:7, 10

Which none of the princes of this world knew: for had they known it, they would not have crucified the LORD of glory.

1 Corinthians 2:8

*　*　*　*

Jehovah, our Righteousness.

Behold, the days come, saith the LORD, that I will raise unto David a righteous Branch, and a King shall reign and prosper, and shall execute judgment and justice in the earth.

In his days Judah shall be saved, and Israel shall dwell safely: and this is his name whereby he shall be called, THE LORD OUR RIGHTEOUSNESS.

Jeremiah 23:5, 6

But of him are ye in Christ Jesus, who of God is made unto us wisdom, and righteousness, and sanctification, and redemption.

1 Corinthians 1:30

*　*　*　*

Jehovah, Above All.

For thou, LORD, art high above all the earth: thou art exalted far above all gods.

Psalm 97:9

But in the last days it shall come to pass, that the mountain of the house of the LORD shall be established in the top of the mountains, and it shall be exalted above the hills; and people shall flow unto it.

222

And I will make her that halted a remnant, and her that was cast far off a strong nation: and the LORD shall reign over them in mount Zion from henceforth, even for ever.

Micah 4:1, 7

He that cometh from above is above all: he that is of the earth is earthly, and speaketh of the earth: he that cometh from heaven is above all.

John 3:31

Jehovah, the First and Last.

Thus saith the LORD the King of Israel, and his redeemer the LORD of hosts; I am the first, and I am the last; and beside me there is no God.

Isaiah 44:6

And when I saw him, I fell at his feet as dead. And he laid his right hand upon me, saying unto me, Fear not; I am the first and the last:

I am he that liveth, and was dead; and, behold, I am alive for evermore, Amen; and have the keys of hell and of death.

Revelation 1:17, 18

* * * *

Hearken unto me, O Jacob and Israel, my called; I am he; I am the first, I also am the last.

Come ye near unto me, hear ye this; I have not spoken in secret from the beginning; from the time that it was, there am I: and now the LORD GOD, and his spirit, hath sent me.

Isaiah 48:12, 16

I am Alpha and Omega, the beginning and the end, the first and the last.

Revelation 22:13

* * * *

Jehovah's Equal.

Awake, O sword, against my shepherd, and against the man that is my fellow, saith the LORD of hosts: smite the shepherd, and the sheep shall be scattered: and I will turn mine hand upon the little ones.

Zechariah 13:7

Let this mind be in you, which was also in Christ Jesus:
Who, being in the form of God, thought it not robbery to be equal with God.

Philippians 2:5, 6

*   *   *   *

Jehovah of Hosts.

And one cried to another, and said, Holy, holy, holy, is the LORD of hosts: the whole earth is full of his glory.

Isaiah 6:3

These things said Esaias, when he saw his glory, and spake of him.

John 12:41

Sanctify the LORD of hosts himself; and let him be your fear, and let him be your dread.

And he shall be for a sanctuary; but for a stone of stumbling and for a rock of offence to both the houses of Israel, for a gin and for a snare to the inhabitants of Jerusalem.

Isaiah 8:13, 14

And a stone of stumbling, and a rock of offence, even to them which stumble at the word, being disobedient: whereunto also they were appointed.

1 Peter 2:8

Jehovah, the Lord.

The LORD said unto my LORD, Sit thou at my right hand, until I make thine enemies thy footstool.

Psalm 110:1

Saying, What think ye of Christ? whose son is he? They say unto him, The son of David.

He saith unto them, How then doth David in spirit call him LORD, saying,

The LORD said unto my LORD, Sit thou on my right hand, till I make thine enemies thy footstool?

224

If David then call him LORD, how is he his son?

* * * *

Jehovah, the Shepherd.

Behold, the LORD GOD will come with strong hand, and his arm shall rule for him: behold, his reward is with him, and his work before him.

He shall feed his flock like a shepherd: he shall gather the lambs with his arm, and carry them in his bosom, and shall gently lead those that are with young.

Isaiah 40:10, 11

Now the God of peace, that brought again from the dead our LORD Jesus, that great shepherd of the sheep, through the blood of the everlasting covenant,

Make you perfect in every good work to do his will, working in you that which is well-pleasing in his sight, through Jesus Christ; to whom be glory for ever and ever. Amen.

Hebrews 13:20, 21

* * * *

Jehovah, the Messenger of the Covenant.

Behold, I will send my messenger, and he shall prepare the way before me: and the LORD, whom ye seek, shall suddenly come to his temple, even the messenger of the covenant, whom ye delight in: behold, he shall come, saith the LORD of hosts.

Malachi 3:1

This is he, of whom it is written, Behold, I send my messenger before thy face, which shall prepare thy way before thee.

Luke 7:27

* * * *

Jehovah, Object of Prayer.

And it shall come to pass, that whosoever shall call on the

name of the LORD shall be delivered: for in mount Zion and in Jerusalem shall be deliverance, as the LORD hath said, and in the remnant whom the LORD shall call.

Joel 2:32

Unto the church of God which is at Corinth, to them that are sanctified in Christ Jesus, called to be saints, with all that in every place call upon the name of Jesus Christ our LORD, both theirs and ours. . .

1 Corinthians 1:2

For whosoever shall call upon the name of the LORD shall be saved.

Romans 10:13

* * * *

Jehovah is One.

Hear, O Israel: The LORD our God is one LORD.

Deuteronomy 6:4

But to us there is but one God, the Father, of whom are all things, and we in him; and one LORD Jesus Christ, by whom are all things, and we by him.

1 Corinthians 8:6

HOW JESUS FULFILLS
THE LEVITICAL FEASTS

PASSOVER, or Unleavened Bread
  (Exodus 12:4-13:10). . .
    THE DEATH OF CHRIST (1 Corinthians 5:7;
                                    Matthew 26:17-20).

PENTECOST, or First Fruits
    (Deuteronomy 16:9-12). . .
    THE RESURRECTION OF JESUS
    (1 Corinthians 15:23), and
    THE OUTPOURING OF THE HOLY SPIRIT
    (Acts 2:1, 4).

TRUMPETS (Numbers 29:1-6). . .
    ISRAEL'S REGATHERING (Matthew 24:31).

DAY OF ATONEMENT, also known as Yom Kippur
    (Leviticus 23:26-32). . .
    CLEANSING BY CHRIST
    (Romans 11:26; Hebrews 9:7).

TABERNACLES, or The Feast of Booths
    (Nehemiah 8:13-18). . .
    REST AND REUNION WITH CHRIST
    (John 7:2).

DEDICATION, also known as The Feast of Lights or
    Hanukkah, (Zechariah 14:16-18). . .
    JESUS IS THE LIGHT OF THE WORLD
    (John 8:12).

PURIM, also known as The Feast of Lots
    (Esther 9:13-18). . .
    JESUS SETS US FREE (John 8:32, 36)

OLD TESTAMENT TYPES
OF THE MESSIAH
(That Were Fulfilled in Jesus)

1. Adam .... Genesis 2:7
   1 Corinthians
2. The Tree of Life .... Genesis 2:9
   John 1:4
3. The Coats of Skin....................... Genesis 3:21
   Hebrews 9:22
4. Abel .... Genesis 2:8-10
   Hebrews 12:24
5. Noah - Comfort .... Genesis 5:28, 29
   2 Corinthians 1:5
6. Noah's Ark .... Genesis 7:13-17
   Hebrews 11:7
7. Abram - Sent of God .... Genesis 12:1-4
   John 10:36, 37
8. Abram - Believed God .... Genesis 15:6
   John 11:41, 42
9. Abram - Obeyed God................... Genesis 12:4
   Hebrews 11:8
10. Abraham - Heir to the .... Genesis 12:7
    Holy Land   Genesis 17:8
                                           Romans 4:13
                                           Genesis 13:15
                                           Galatians 3:16
                                           Ezekiel 27:21
                                           Matthew 19:28
11. Abraham - To Be a .... Genesis 27:18
    Blessing to the Gentiles   Acts 3:25
12. Abraham - God's friend................. Isaiah 41:8
    Matthew 17:5
13. Melchizedek .... Genesis 14:18-20
    Psalm 110:4
    Hebrews 7:1-17
14. Isaac offered up .... Genesis 22:2-12
    Hebrews 11:17-19
15. The Ram took Isaac's place .... Genesis 22:13
    Isaiah 53:6
    1 Corinthians 15:3
16. Isaac the Peacemaker .... Genesis 22:19-22
    Ephesians 2:14-17

36. The Morning & Evening Sacrifices	Exodus 29:38, 39 John 1:29
37. The Whole Burnt Offering	Leviticus 1:3, 4, 13 Hebrews 10:10
38. The Peace Offering	Leviticus 3:1, 2 Ephesians 2:14-18
39. The Sin Offering	Leviticus 4:2-12 Hebrews 13:11-13
40. The Leper's Cleansing	Leviticus 14:6, 7 Hebrews 10:21-23
41. The Day of Atonement	Leviticus 16:15-34 Hebrews 9:11, 12
42. The Ransom	Numbers 3:11-13 Hosea 13:14 Matthew 20:25-28
43. The Red Heifer	Numbers 19:2-9 Hebrews 9:13, 14
44. The Tabernacle	Exodus 40:33, 34 Colossians 2:9
45. The Ark of the Covenant	Exodus 25:16 Psalm 40:7, 8 John 15:10 Luke 22:20
46. The Mercy Seat	Exodus 25:21, 22 Romans 3:25 Hebrews 4:16
47. The Veil of the Tabernacle & Temple	Exodus 40:21 2 Chronicles 3:14 Hebrews 10:9, 10
48. The Golden Altar	Exodus 40:26, 27 Hebrews 13:15
49. The Table and Shewbread	Exodus 25:23-30 John 6:48
50. The Golden Lamp-stand	Exodus 25:31 John 8:12
51. The Laver of Brass	Exodus 30:18-20 Zechariah 13:1 John 13:3-10
52. The Brazen Altar	Exodus 27:1, 2 Hebrews 13:10
53. The Brazen Serpent	Numbers 21:9 John 3:14, 15
54. The Cities of Refuge	Numbers 35:6 Hebrews 6:18

55. Joshua, the Commander	Joshua 1:5, 6 Isaiah 55:3, 4 Hebrews 2:10
56. Joshua, the Overcomer	Joshua 11:23 John 16:33
57. Joshua, the Rest-giver	Joshua 11:23 Joshua 22:4 Matthew 11:28
58. Gideon, Sent by Jehovah	Judges 6:14 John 10:36
59. Samson	Judges 16:30 Colossians 2:14, 15
60. David, a man after God's own heart	1 Samuel 13:14 Matthew 3:17
61. David, a Shepherd	1 Samuel 16:11-13 John 10:11
62. David, the Giant-killer	1 Samuel 17:50 Genesis 3:15 Hebrews 2:14
63. David, Exalted by Jehovah	Psalm 89:19-21
64. David, King of Israel	2 Samuel 8:15 Matthew 27:11
65. Jonathan, the Friend	1 Samuel 20:42 Proverbs 18:24
66. Solomon, David's Royal Son	2 Samuel 7:12 Luke 1:32, 33
67. Solomon the Wisest Man	1 Kings 4:30, 31
68. Solomon, the Builder of God's Temple	1 Kings 6:1, 14 1 Peter 2:5
69. Solomon's Temple	1 Kings 8:10, 11 John 2:18-22
70. Jonah's 3 days in the Great Fish	Jonah 1:17 Matthew 12:40
71. Jonah, the Foreign Missionary	Jonah 3:1-5 Matthew 12:41

NAMES FOR GOD

JEHOVAH . . . . (YHWH, pronounced Yah'-way)
I Am, or He which is, or He
who is truly present; Self-
existent (Exodus 3:15)

JEHOVAH-JIREH . . . . . Yahweh will see, or Yahweh will
provide (Genesis 22:14)

JEHOVAH-NISSI . . . . . Jehovah is my banner, or
Jehovah is my standard
(Exodus 17:15)

JEHOVAH-SHALOM . . Yahweh is peace (Judges 6:23)

JEHOVAH- . . . . Yahweh is there
SHAMMAH (Ezekiel 48:35)

JEHOVAH-SABOATH . The Lord of Hosts
(Malachi 1:14)

JEHOVAH-RAAH . . . . . The Lord, My Shepherd
(Psalm 23:1)

JEHOVAH- . . . . The Lord Sanctifies
MEKODDISHKEM (Exodus 31:13)

JEHOVAH-TSIDKENU The Lord, Our Righteousness
(Jeremiah 23:6)

JEHOVAH-RAPHA . . . The Lord that Heals
(Exodus 15:27)

ELOHIM . . . . God, the general name for God;
also means "mighty" or
"strong" (Deuteronomy 4:35)

EL SHADDAI . . . . God of the Mountain, or God
Almighty, All Sufficient
(Genesis 17:1; Exodus 6:3)

EL 'ELYON . . . . God Almighty, or Most High
God (Genesis 14:18-24)

EL 'OLAM . . . . God of Eternity (Genesis 21:33)

EL RO'I . . . . God the Seeing one, or God
who sees me, or God of Seeing
(Genesis 16:13)

EL RAHUM . . . . God of Compassion
(Deuteronomy 4:31)

EL NOSE' . . . . God of Forgiveness
(Psalm 99:8)

EL HANNUN . . . . God of Grace (Nehemiah 9:31)

EL KANNA' . . . . The jealous God (Exodus 20:5)

OTHER FREQUENT TERMS
FOR GOD

1. God .... (tsur - 'rock') Isaiah 44:8

2. God .... (theos) used throughout New
   Testament

3. Lord .... (kurios, in Greek; adonai, in
   Hebrew)

4. Holy One .... (of Israel) (qadosh) Psalm 71:22
   and throughout Old Testament

5. Mighty One .... (el) Psalm 50:1 (gibbor)
   Deuteronomy 10:17

6. Light giver .... (Maor) Genesis 1:16

7. Father .... (ab) Psalm 89:26 and throughout
   Old Testament

8. Judge .... (shaphat) Genesis 18:25

9. Redeemer .... (gaal) Job 19:25

10. Saviour .... (yasha) Isaiah 43:3

11. Deliverer .... (palat) Psalm 18:2

12. Shield, Buckler .... (magen) Psalm 3:3

13. Strength .... (eyaluth) Psalm 22:19

14. Righteous One .... (tsaddiq) Psalm 7:9

15. Lord of Hosts .... (elohim tsebhaoth) Jeremiah 11:20

THE MESSIANIC PSALMS

1. Psalm 2   The Glory of the Eternal Son
2. Psalm 40   The Incarnation
3. Psalm 91   The Temptation
4. Psalm 41   The Betrayal
5. Psalm 22   The Crucifixion
6. Psalm 69   The Tresspass Offering
7. Psalm 16   The Resurrection
8. Psalm 68   The Ascension
9. Psalm 45   The King-Bridegroom
10. Psalm 24   The King of Glory
11. Psalm 110   The Priest-King-Judge
12. Psalm 8   The Last Adam
13. Psalm 72   The Millenial Reign
14. Psalm 89   The Davidic Covenant
15. Psalm 102   The Unchangeable One
16. Psalm 118   The Cornerstone

Other Psalms with Messianic Overtones

PSALMS: 17, 18, 19, 20, 21, 23, 24, 42, 43, 44, 46, 47, 48, 67, 69, 70
71, 85, 87, 90, 94, 95, 96, 97, 98, 99, 100, 101, 103,
107, 108, 109, 111, 112, 113, 122, 123, 124, 125, 126,
132.

INSPIRATIONAL LIBRARY

Beautiful purse/pocket size editions of Christian Classics bound in flexible leatherette or genuine Bonded Leather. The Bonded Leather editions have gold edges and make beautiful gifts.

THE BIBLE PROMISE BOOK Over 1000 promises from God's Word arranged by topic. What does the Bible promise about matters like: Anger, Illness, Jealousy, Sex, Money, Old Age, et cetera, et cetera.

Flexible Leatherette . . . . $ 3.95
Genuine Bonded Leather $10.95

DAILY LIGHT One of the most popular daily devotionals with readings for both morning and evening. One page for each day of the year.

Flexible Leatherette . . . . $ 4.95
Genuine Bonded Leather $10.95

WISDOM FROM THE BIBLE Daily thoughts from the Proverbs which communicate truth about ourselves and the world around us. One page for each day in the year.

Flexible Leatherette . . . . $ 4.95
Genuine Bonded Leather $10.95

MY DAILY PRAYER JOURNAL Each page is dated and has a Scripture verse and ample room for you to record your thoughts, prayers and praises. One page for each day of the year.

Flexible Leatherette . . . . $ 4.95
Genuine Bonded Leather $10.95

Available wherever books are sold.

or order from:

Barbour and Company, Inc.
164 Mill Street   Box 1219
Westwood, New Jersey   07675